The

# DEATH

of the

# *CUSTODIAN*

the case of the missing tutor

by
W. Carl Ketcherside

A Division of Standard Publishing
Cincinnati, Ohio
**40036**

**Library of Congress Catalog Card No. 75-32003**
**ISBN: 0-87239-035-7**

## PREFACE

I doubt that a lot of authors really know what made them write their books. That may be a good thing, otherwise some writers would never be able to live with their own consciences. This little book is different. I know why I wrote it, although its content represents a viewpoint in direct contradiction to what I would have expressed a few years ago. Like so many others who believe in Christ, as I grew older and was able to form more mature judgments, I became more aware and discerning of the meaning of grace. It was this new insight which made such an inward change in my life and it clamored for expression.

Even at that, I probably would not have written had it not been that I met A. V. Mansur, a retired dry-land farmer who lives in California. Mr. Mansur and his wife are quiet and reserved, living modestly and simply, away from what the poet calls "the madding throng's ignoble strife." But they are meditative and contemplative. Their early life of toil taught them much about our relationship to, and our dependence upon, the Creator of the universe.

A deepening penetration of the revelation of God encouraged Mr. Mansur to feel that in Christ we are freed from enslavement to law, that God no longer relates to His people upon the basis of their conformity to a written code. This demanded a refocusing of the apostolic letters and re-examination of the very nature of the "new covenant," referred to in Hebrews 8:7-13. Fortunately, it was about this time that I began stating my growing convictions along the same lines, and my California friend and brother urged me to place them in a more permanent and useful form. This book is the result.

If you are benefited in your reading of this little thesis, you must give any glory and praise to Him "whom having not seen we love." Certainly the writer and the one who encouraged him to write can take little credit. Neither one can lay claim to any profundity or erudition, and both are content to be simply slaves of Jesus.

In 1706, the philosopher, John Locke, wrote, "Reading furnishes the mind only with materials of knowledge; it is thinking makes what we read ours." This book intends only to share building blocks of thought. It is hoped they will prove helpful in your construction of a life worthy of the divine call.

*W. Carl Ketcherside*

# CONTENTS

"The law was our custodian until Christ came, that we might be justified by faith. But now that faith has come, we are no longer under a custodian."

—Galatians 3:24, 25; RSV

Chapter 1

# THE GOD OF COVENANTS

Daniel Webster, who was born in New Hampshire in 1782, became one of the most eloquent orators ever to grace the American scene. His orations helped to launch him upon a career of public service which carried him to the United States Senate, and made him Secretary of State under three presidents.

On one occasion, Mr. Webster was asked to state the most important thought that ever occurred to his mind. His reply was simple and pointed. "The most important thought I ever had," he said, "was that of my individual responsibility to God."

If this was the most important thought to lodge in such a brilliant brain, perhaps all of us should ponder it carefully and honestly. It would be well for us to explore the nature of God's relationship with man as revealed in the Bible. This will help us to understand the mercy of God, and why we are not under law, but under grace.

In the orderly process of creation, when God had formed the material universe, He said, "Come now, let us make man in our

9

own image." It is apparent from subsequent Scriptural disclosures, that this statement was addressed to the Living Word who was with God and was God (John 1:1). Concerning the Word it was said, "All things were made through him, and without him was not anything made that was made" (John 1:3; RSV).

The "image of God" had no reference to man's physical frame. Man bears the image of God because he is a rational, intelligent, and creative personality. It is the spirit, not the clay dwelling of the spirit, which bears the imprint of the divine image. When man was created, God declared that it was not good for man to be alone. By his very nature man is a social being. His personality develops best by association with others of his own kind. So God made a helpmeet worthy of man and presented her to him as a companion.

At the same time the family relationship was instituted by a divine decree. God said, "For this cause shall a man leave father and mother, and shall cleave to his wife: and they twain shall be one flesh" (Matthew 19:5; KJV). As a place for the pair to dwell a garden was created eastward in Eden, and man was assigned the task of overseeing it and keeping it trim and neat. It was here that God placed the first limitation upon the primeval pair. He granted them permission to eat of the fruit of every tree in the garden except one. The tree of knowledge of good and evil was off limits. God said, "You shall not eat of it, for the day you eat of it you will die."

The rest of the story is well known. Satan, adopting the form of the serpent, enticed the woman by the lust of the flesh, the lust of the eye, and the pride of life. She ate of the forbidden fruit and gave it to her husband, who also ate of it. Sin thus entered the world. The effect was seen immediately. The man and woman, enveloped in a sense of shame, sought to hide from the presence of God. Several thousand years later Paul summed up the consequences by saying, "Sin came into the world through one man and death through sin, and so death spread to all men because all men sinned" (Romans 5:12; RSV).

In order to preclude the possibility that man would eat of the tree of life and live forever in a state of alienation and disgrace, God ejected Adam and Eve from the paradise in which He had placed them. But even at the beginning there was a ray of hope penetrating the darkness of despair. In pronouncing a sentence of degradation upon the serpent, God said, "I will put enmity between thee and the woman, and between thy seed and her seed; it shall bruise thy head, and thou shalt bruise his heel" (KJV). The head of the serpent is the seat of his power. The venom in his fangs produces

11

death. The time would come when the seed of the woman, although bruised by the serpent, would destroy or crush the one who had power over death.

The world of mankind had to pass through stages of development similar to those of the individuals who composed it. The world had its infancy, childhood, and adolescence, before it attained maturity. Just as parents must accommodate their instruction, training, and discipline to the state of their children at a given time, so God likewise had to adjust His requirements to the condition of humanity in progressive phases.

A realization of this fact leads to certain inevitable conclusions. Things that might be condoned in one age could not be continued in another. We smile at the antics of a little child, but realize that the same actions on the part of an older person would be an occasion for regret and reproof. The principle of human responsibility is stated by the apostle Paul to the Athenian philosophers in the statement, "The times of ignorance God overlooked, but now he commands all men everywhere to repent" (Acts 17:30; RSV).

God has never required of man in any age what he is unable to perform. He has always adjusted His mandates to meet the needs and abilities of man in the circumstances in which he is found. A good

12

illustration of this is found in what may be termed "the evolution of the demonstration of worship." Certainly the God who is "over all, through all, and in all," has the right, and even the obligation, of revealing what is acceptable as worship of His majesty at any time.

When man lived in a nomadic culture, he was required to offer sacrifices upon an altar consisting of an earthen mound. When certain geographical spots became hallowed because of significant events, a more permanent altar of field stones was permitted. However, to avoid any temptation to idolatry, all engraving or carving upon the face of the stones was forbidden (Exodus 20:24, 25). Later, when God separated a people from bondage to form a nation, He provided for them a tent, or tabernacle, suitable to their wandering life for forty years in the wilderness.

When this same people settled in a land that was to become their own, God selected a city where He inscribed His name. Here they were permitted to erect a house, the magnificence of which was unsurpassed in its day. In spite of its lavish beauty and splendor, it was to provide only a temporary place for adoration of God. At the dedication service, the king who supervised and financed its erection acknowledged that it could never qualify as a dwelling for God (2 Chronicles 6:18).

When Jesus came into the world to share the human lot, He made it clear that the worship of God was not to be limited by time or place. " 'Neither on this mountain nor in Jerusalem will you worship the Father. God is spirit, and those who worship him must worship in spirit and truth' " (John 4:21, 24; RSV). God now has no holy places, holy days, or holy things. All of these belong to a childhood age that we should have outgrown. God now has only a holy people. The only sanctuary is a consecrated human heart. The only temple is the one composed of living stones. Those who dedicate piles of brick and stone, and speak in awed tones of "the sanctuary" are spiritually infantile. They have not "put away childish things."

There is but one more step awaiting. There remains a new Jerusalem to be revealed. John, who was given a preview of the city, wrote, "I saw no temple therein" (Revelation 21:22; KJV). No other observation more fully conveys the difference between life on our material planet and that in the eternal state. There is not a city upon earth that does not contain edifices devoted to worship. In the city of the Ultimate there will be no place of worship. There the temple at last becomes divinely personal: "For the Lord God Almighty and the Lamb are the temple of it."

Responsibility is always gauged by man's

ability to respond. God has revealed His will progressively, as man was able to grasp it and fulfill it. Human responsibility was thus judged upon the basis of man's place in history at the time. Yet there is one fact about the divine-human relationship which is always the same. This fact is that God has chosen to relate to man on the basis of covenants. He is a covenant-making God. No one who ignores this fact will ever fully grasp God's plan and purpose in any age.

God's covenants with man are always acts of divine grace. They stem from the fact that God is love, and it is the nature of this love to be ever active and outgoing toward its object. There is no obligation owed to sinful man to compel the Creator to continue to act toward him in such a manner as to promote his welfare. The covenants of God grow out of the nature of God, and not out of the nature of man.

A simple covenant is an agreement between two parties. In a human covenant the party of the first part and the party of the second part are equals before the law. This cannot be the case in a divine-human covenant, however. God always must be regarded as supreme. He is sovereign in the universe. He proposes and man accepts. Man is in no position to bargain with God or to sue for better terms.

While God proposes terms of His covenants, He never imposes them. Man is free to refuse the proffered relationship when it is conditional. In most instances a sign or seal of the covenant is provided. Such a visible token serves as a constant reminder of the relationship. Like a wedding ring, it is a symbol of a covenant in force, to both those who were parties to the covenant and those who were not.

As a working basis for continued study, let us summarize with the statement of two facts that are apparent to every person who is informed in the revelation of God. These will be foundational for all else that is deduced from the sacred Scriptures.

1. *Covenant Relationship.* God has chosen to relate to mankind on the basis of covenants. All of God's covenants with man have been designed to achieve the good of humanity. God has revealed himself as a covenant-making God. He has entered into agreements based upon His perfect character. He has placed himself on record by making immutable promises. The fact that one covenant supersedes another is not attributable to fickleness or caprice, but to the changing condition of the world of mankind. Our relationship to God must be a covenantal one. We must enter such an agreement freely as the party of the second part. It is a profound truth that the infinite Creator respects the sovereignty of the human will, to the extent that the created

may reject the Creator. Finite man may refuse the hand that made him, but he cannot refuse the consequences that follow.

2. *Rules or Ordinances.* God has arranged that all of the blessings and privileges He confers upon men shall be enjoyed in conjunction with ordinances of His own appointment. This is true in both the natural and spiritual realms. Thus we read of the ordinances of the sun, moon, and stars in Jeremiah 31:35, 36. The same word is employed here for "ordinances" as is used for expressions of worship. One might as well try to secure light in the material realm without the sun and moon as to seek for light in the spiritual domain without God's revelation.

The primitive root from which "ordinance" is derived, literally means "to hack." It referred first to the action of cutting messages and directions in the bark of trees. Then it came to refer to the action of carving in stone slabs or pillars by use of a chisel and hammer. It is significant that the words of the Ten Commandments were written in stone tablets by the finger of God, the Holy Spirit. The word finally progressed until it meant "to engrave." Laws and enactments were originally chiseled in stone, and later scratched or engraved in metal plates. Thus, the term eventually came to mean an enactment or appointment, generally by proper authority. God's blessings are in response to God's ordinances.

With this introductory and background material we can examine the initial covenant God introduced and preserved in the Scriptural record. It will be confusing to refer to God's commandment with Noah as "the first covenant." That term was appropriated by a divine writer and applied to a later covenant enacted to create a special nation out of former slaves. That nation was designed to keep alive on earth the concept of monotheism, that is, belief in one God (Cp. Hebrews 8:7, 11). The initial covenant was made with Noah. It was the first in point of time, but not the first in terms of importance to the purpose of God. A study of it, however, will lay the groundwork for investigation of other covenants of God.

# Chapter 2

# THE COVENANT WITH NOAH

The word "antediluvian" has been given to the age before the flood. It simply means "preceding the deluge." It was an age saturated with gross iniquity. There were two strains of humanity then in existence. The descendants of Seth called themselves by the name of the Lord. They were "sons of God." The descendants of Cain were loose and dissolute men. The two families mingled in marriage. Their offspring became violent, and as a result, wickedness was great in the earth. Every imagination of the thoughts of human hearts was evil continually, and the Lord was sorry He had made man. It grieved Him in His heart. He declared, " 'I will blot out man whom I have created from the face of the ground, man and beast and creeping things and birds of the air, for I am sorry that I have made them' " (Genesis 6:7; RSV).

There was one exception, a man by the name of Noah. He is introduced with two remarkable statements. The first reads, "But Noah found grace in the eyes of the Lord" (v. 8). The second says, "Noah was a

19

just man and perfect in his generations, and Noah walked with God" (vv. 8, 9). This is the first time the word "grace" is used in the Bible, and Noah was the first man to be called "just."

The original Hebrew word for "grace" is one that suggests an active personal principle manifesting itself, not in a mere attitude, but in deed. It is not an abstract quality but a vital demonstration. It may be properly defined as a free bestowal of kindness upon another who does not deserve the blessing, and has no means of adequately paying for it. God looked upon Noah with favor, which manifested itself in the provision for his escape from the determined destruction.

The word "just" is akin to the word for "righteousness," and this is a word of relationship. Noah had kept himself free from the contamination of the social culture. He walked with God instead of with the world. A direct descendant of Seth, he had kept his association pure. He was "blameless in his generation" (RSV). God disclosed to Noah His determination to make an end of all flesh because violence reigned in the earth. Probation was to be extended for 120 years, during which time Noah was to construct an ark.

The means chosen to purge the earth was a cleansing bath of water. Since every nation of antiquity has its tradition of the flood, this may account for the almost universal ritual employment of water as a symbol for purification. After more than a year in the ark, Noah and his family stepped forth into a new world. Noah's first act was to construct an altar. In the role of patriarchal priest he offered sacrifices of every clean beast and bird. The sacrificial odor pleased the Lord, who vowed never again to destroy every living creature as He had done. The lifetime of the earth would be an undisturbed continuity.

Noah and his sons now constituted God's sole representatives for the population of the new world. Accordingly, they were given the identical responsibility conferred originally upon Adam. "Be fruitful, and multiply, and replenish the earth" (Genesis 1:28; 9:1; KJV).

The first recorded covenant that God made with the world of His creation, was a covenant including every creature in whose nostrils was the breath of life. God informed Noah and his sons that He would establish His covenant with them and their descendants, and with the birds, cattle, and every beast of the earth, that had come out of the ark. The fact that God included all these in a covenant should give us deep concern about endangered species.

The terms of the covenant were plainly announced: " 'I establish my covenant with you, that never again shall all flesh be cut off by the waters of a flood, and never again shall there be a flood to destroy the earth' " (Genesis 9:11; RSV). The duration of the covenant was fixed for "all future generations." Thus it was designated "an everlasting covenant" (Genesis 9:16).

The Hebrew word for "everlasting" is *olam*. It is one of several terms signifying duration. In its origin it signified veiling or concealing from sight. Gradually it came to mean that which extended beyond one's vision, and finally developed the connotation of "age-lasting." To determine the extent of the duration one must study the limitations that appear in the context. In this instance they are clearly given. The covenant is to stand while the earth remains, or while the descendants of Noah in all future generations remain upon the earth.

A visible sign of the covenant was given, which would be observable for its duration. God said, "I do set my bow in the cloud, and it shall be for a token of a covenant between me and the earth" (Genesis 9:13). God nowhere says that the bow is to bring to man's remembrance that a flood will never again destroy the earth. Instead, God said, " 'When I bring clouds over the earth and the bow is seen in the clouds, I will remember my covenant' " (Genesis 9:14, 15; RSV). Thus the bow is not so much a reminder to us of the agreement as it is a sign of God's covenant faithfulness. As such a symbol we may expect it to recur in any circumstances where the divine fidelity is to be displayed. For this reason, the rainbow is used in conjunction with the throne of God (Cp. Revelation 4:3).

Inasmuch as this is the initial or first covenant God made with man, we should study it carefully for any indication of the manner of God's dealings on a covenant basis. We can readily see that He arranged no preceding consultation with man as to the content or terms of the covenant. The proposal was not, therefore, an outgrowth of reasoning between the divine and human minds. The covenant was an arrangement conceived by God alone, in His infinite and infallible mind. It was revealed or disclosed to man. This is important, since we tend to think of a covenant as growing out of mutual arbitration.

History is a record of the footprints of God in the life of humanity. The two most outstanding events of divine interposition in the affairs of the world were the flood and the incarnation. Of such transcendent significance was the first that it stands as a constant rebuke to those skeptics who deny the possibility of a termination of the present world order, based upon a false assumption of continuity in the natural realm since creation (2 Peter 3:3, 4). The second made such an impact that it changed the calendar. It was as if time stood still, then resumed with a new meaning.

In the flood God demonstrated His wrath; in the coming of Jesus He manifested His love. "Behold therefore the goodness and severity of God: on them which fell, severity; but toward thee, goodness" (Romans 11:22; KJV). The first event was a visitation of destruction; the second, of salvation. The one was to terminate life; the other that it might be granted more abundantly.

Both covenants were given through a comforter. The first was given through Noah, whose name means "comforter" (Genesis 5:29). The second was given through the Holy Spirit as a Comforter from the Father. Because of the original covenant we need never fear the destruction of all flesh by water; because of the last we need never fear the second death. The covenant with Noah resulted in a rainbow spanning the clouds of the heavens; the covenant of grace has its rainbow round about the throne of Him who will come in the clouds of Heaven. The God of the universe is revealed as a covenant-making God.

Our relationship with God must be on the basis of a covenant. As finite creatures seeking to please Him, we must investigate and become aware of the implications growing out of this fact.

Chapter 3

# THE COVENANT WITH ABRAHAM

When Noah and his sons came out of the ark they faced a new world. A fresh start had to be made. Accordingly, they were given a repetition of the primal commission. "And God blessed Noah and his sons, and said to them, 'Be fruitful and multiply, and fill the earth' " (Genesis 9:1; RSV). The oldest ethnographic chart known to man is found in Genesis 10. It details the nations that came from Shem, Ham, and Japheth. It closes with the observation, "These are the families of the sons of Noah, according to their genealogies, in their nations; and from these the nations spread abroad on the earth after the flood" (Genesis 10:32; RSV).

In the next chapter, although certainly not in chronological order, is inserted a rather detailed account of how the dispersion was accomplished. At the time "the whole earth had one language and few words," (Genesis 11:1; RSV). Apparently, under the influence of Nimrod, a descendant of Ham, the people decided to resist being scattered. They resolved to construct a city and erect a high tower as a visible rallying point. In order to do this they fired bricks which they cemented together with bitumen, or asphalt. The place chosen was the plain of Shinar.

The power exerted in working together and in speaking the same things was attested to by God, who declared, " 'Behold, they are one people, and they have all one language; and this is only the beginning of what they will do; and nothing that they propose to do will now be impossible for them' " (v. 6; RSV). To overthrow the conspiracy calculated to avoid populating the earth, God said, " 'Come, let us go down, and there confuse their language, that they may not understand one another's speech' " (v. 7; RSV). The record adds, "So the Lord scattered them abroad from there over the face of all the earth, and they left off building the city." The "so" shows how it was done. It means "in this manner," or "by this method."

It is well to note that the descendants of Arpachshad and Eber, of the family of Shem, settled in that area along the Euphrates River which came to be designated "the land of the Chaldeans." It was not long until the tribes of mankind, seeking an outlet for the worshiping instinct, degenerated into idolatry, paying homage to both natural and artificial gods. The idea of one God, Maker of Heaven and earth, was fast disappearing beneath the weight of superstition and tradition. It became obvious that, if the concept of monotheism was to survive, it would have to be made the sacred trust of a particular nation, around which such safeguards could be constructed as to segregate it from the rest of humanity, with its contaminating influence.

Thus, when every nation on earth had chosen gods for itself, the God of Heaven chose for himself a nation on earth. To sire this select people, He chose an Arpachshadean from the city of Ur, whose name was Abram. *Ab* is the Hebrew for "father," and *ram* is the word for "high" or "chief." The very name signifies that its bearer was a man of destiny, one who was to be an outstanding progenitor.

Abram was the son of Terah, an idol worshiper, whose father, Nahor, had also served other gods (Joshua 24:2). Abram was instructed to leave his country, kindred, and father's house. While he obeyed with alacrity the command to go, he did not at first fully comply with the conditions. He and Sarai, his wife, accompanied his father and nephew, "and they went forth together from Ur of the Chaldeans to go into the land of Canaan; but when they came to Haran, they settled there" (Genesis 11:31; RSV). This delayed Abram until after the decease of his father. Then

27

"Abram took Sarai his wife, and Lot his brother's son, and all their possessions which they had gathered, and the persons that they had gotten in Haran; and they set forth to go into the land of Canaan" (12:5; RSV).

They entered Canaan, later called Palestine, or "land of the Philistines" from the north. Since they were a band of nomads, they wandered southward as their animals found grazing to sustain them. Abram built an altar to the Lord, to mark every principal stop. Driven into Egypt by a serious famine, they sojourned there until sustenance was again found in Canaan. "So Abram went up from Egypt, he and his wife, and all that he had, and Lot with him, into the Negeb" (13:1; RSV).

A quarrel among the herdsmen was settled by an agreement between Abram and Lot to go their several ways. Lot chose the verdant plains of Jordan and removed to Sodom. This divested Abram of the last of his relatives. He was now separated from his kindred. It is appropriate that we note the words of the Lord immediately forthcoming. "The Lord said unto Abram, after that Lot was separated from him, Lift up now thine eyes, and look from the place where thou art northward, and southward, and eastward, and westward: for all the land which thou seest, to thee will I give it, and to thy seed for ever" (13:14, 15; KJV).

Why did the Lord select this one individual from the multitude of men upon the earth, to be the progenitor of His mighty nation? Every nation began with one man whose offspring became a clan, then a tribe, and eventually a nation. What was the outstanding characteristic of Abram that made him the subject of God's choice? Concerning this choice it is affirmed that God "calleth those things which be not as though they were" (Romans 4:17; KJV). James declared, "Known unto God are all his works from the beginning of the world" (Acts 15:18; KJV). It appears that Abram, of all men on earth in his day, possessed that one quality which commended him to the Lord as the progenitor of a covenant people, whose relationship would be established upon the basis of faith.

In order to bring mankind up to that state of maturity where a covenant based upon faith could be operative and effective, it became necessary to make another covenant with Abram that could provide the background and setting for the last and greatest agreement to be made with man. Thus there were two covenants embraced in the promises to Abram. One was fleshly and temporal, and its token was a sign in the flesh. Its promises were carnal. The other was spiritual and lasting. Its promises were of a better and a more enduring nature. One of these covenants was not a continuation of the other, although the first provided a frame of reference for the second. They were addressed to different persons for different purposes. Unless this is kept in mind, one will become involved in serious error.

## A COVENANT AFTER THE FLESH

In his beautiful allegory to the vacillating Galatians, the apostle Paul says, "For these are the two covenants" (4:24; KJV). He distinguishes the subjects of the two by the expressions "born after the flesh" and "by the promise." It is true that he was dealing with the covenants made at literal Mount Sinai and figurative Mount Sion, but the covenant at Sinai was a national one conferred upon the physical seed of Abram. It was merely a ratification on a national basis of the original one given at a time when Abram had not one child. Before the Lord could make a "kingdom of priests," and a "holy nation" (Exodus 19:6; KJV), he had first to provide seed for the primal covenantee. This was a remarkable arrangement in itself, considering that Abram was "about an hundred years old," and reproductively his body and Sarai's womb were dead (Romans 4:19).

When God called Abram, He assured him, "I will make of thee a great nation, and I will bless thee, and make thy name great; and thou shalt be a blessing: and I will bless them that bless thee, and curse him that curseth thee: and in thee shall all families of the earth be blessed" (Genesis 12:2, 3; KJV). Here, at the very beginning, we have the germ of both covenants, and it will be noted that both are to be realized through the seed of Abraham. National greatness and universal blessing—these are the attainments to be achieved.

To those who are of the opinion that these words were spoken to Abram while he sojourned in Haran, we merely remark that Stephen said, "The God of glory appeared unto our father Abraham, when he was in Mesopotamia, before he dwelt in Charran" (Acts 7:2; KJV). The same speaker also says relative to Canaan, "He promised that he would give it to him for a possession, and to his seed after him, when as yet he had no child" (v. 5; KJV). This last fact presented a concern to both Abram and Sarai, although their reactions were different.

Sarai devised an expedient, suggesting that Abram have sexual congress with Hagar, her Egyptian maidservant, saying, "It may be that I may obtain children by her" (Genesis 16:2; KJV). Hagar bore a son, who was named Ishmael, and he became the illustrious head of twelve tribes, now represented by the Arabs. Later, when

Sarai's own son was born, enmity existed between the two. That hostility between their seed still makes the headlines of our metropolitan newspapers regularly.

Abram had concluded that his trusted homeborn servant, Eliezer of Damascus, would be adopted and become his heir, in lieu of natural seed, and he so informed the Lord (Genesis 15:2, 3). But the Lord assured him such was not in the divine plan. His heir would be an offspring of Sarai and himself. Then occurred a demonstration that was remarkable and must have made a lifelong impression upon the patriarch.

Abram was taken outside his tent before dawn and directed to look toward Heaven. He was told that this progeny would be as innumerable as the stars shimmering in the still darkened sky. It was at this juncture the record declares, "And he believed in the Lord; and he counted it to him for righteousness" (15:6; KJV). To this important statement we will have to make frequent allusion. This is the first time the word "believe" occurs in the sacred record. Abraham was indeed "the father of the faithful."

The Lord said to Abram, "I am the Lord that brought thee out of Ur of the Chaldees, to give thee this land to inherit it" (v. 7). When Abram asked by what means he could be certain of the inheritance, the Lord told him to provide a heifer, a female goat, and a ram, each three years old, also a turtledove and a young pigeon. It will be recognized that these constitute the representative categories of sacrificial birds and animals.

Abram killed all of these and split the animals in two, laying each half over against the other, leaving a passageway between. In Jeremiah 34:18 we are informed that this was a solemn way of ratifying a covenant. The parties to the covenant killed an animal, dividing the carcass lengthwise. They placed the pieces opposite each other and walked between them to meet in the middle, where they took the ritual oath. In effect, the oath was a plea for the one who broke the covenant to suffer the same fate as the slain animal.

Abram kept birds of prey off the slain beasts all day. At sunset he fell into a supernatural trance. He heard the voice of God speaking and saw a smoking furnace and burning lamp pass between the pieces of animals, symbolizing that God was entering into a covenant. The record says, "In the same day the Lord made a covenant with Abram, saying, Unto thy seed have I given this land" (Genesis 15:18; KJV). A description of the boundaries and the names of the nations inhabiting the territory was then provided. This closed a memorable day. It began before dawn and lasted until after dark. Abram had learned that his heir would be personally begotten, and that his seed would be granted the whole land of Canaan. All history after this was affected by this covenant.

## THE DIVINE PURPOSE

It would be well for us to study God's purpose in the covenant, as it is related to the land inheritance of the fleshly seed of Abram. The divine intent was to constitute a nation for the preservation of the great truth of the existence of one God. That is why the nation began with one who believed in God with such intensity of purpose that his very faith could be "counted unto him for righteousness" in the sight of God.

But the faith of an ancestor was not enough. It was essential to establish the nation that came from his loins in a territory of their own, to segregate them by law, custom, practice, and geography from other nations that were steeped in polytheism. It is difficult, if not impossible, to build a strong central power out of nomadic herdsmen, whose tendency is to be ever on the move and who prefer dwelling in the desert to living in the city.

Accordingly, God ordained for these people to become slaves in the most enlightened nation of that day. Here the wanderlust was burned out of them. They were taught by compulsion to make bricks. They learned the discipline of daily toil. They were forced to construct great cities such as Pithom and Raamses. So effective was the attempt to make them a settled people that when they were finally led forth into the wilderness, they longingly sought to return to the land of slavery.

Since every nation in that day was idolatrous, during the period of serfdom the descendants of Abraham were exposed to idolatrous practices. These were made abhorrent by virtue of an edict of the Pharaoh that all of their male children should be sacrificed to the maw of the chief god, the Nile River. Moreover, when the time of deliverance came, great catastrophes fell upon both the heathen inhabitants and their gods of lower animal life. The superiority of the God of Israel was clearly demonstrated. God promised, " 'I will pass through the land of Egypt that night, and I will smite all the firstborn in the land of Egypt, both man and beast; and on all the gods of Egypt I will execute judgment: I am the Lord' " (Exodus 12:12; RSV). Deliverance began with fearful judgment from the Lord upon the helpless gods of mighty Egypt. This night, which was memorialized for all future generations by a feast, served as a constant rebuke against idolatry.

The land of Canaan was peculiarly adapted to the divine purpose. It was selected from the lands of the earth, as Abram had been from the inhabitants of the earth, and as Israel was from the nations. As the seed of Abram became the people of God, so Palestine became the land of the Lord (Psalm 85:1; Isaiah 8:8). The land could not even be sold on a permanent basis. It did not belong to man to convey. As Israel became a holy people, so this territory became "the holy land" (Zechariah 2:12).

This territory was situated in a strategic position to accomplish the will of God. It was bounded on the north by the towering Lebanon Range, on the east by the Jordan River, on the south by the Wilderness of Sin, and on the west by the Mediterranean Sea. Even more remotely sealed in by the Arabian Desert, it provided for the compact dwelling of a people around the center of their worship. Yet it was also on the main trade routes, along which flowed the commerce of the ancient world.

The purpose of God with regard to the seed of Abraham was to keep intact the notion of one God. The ultimate design was to bring all nations to an acknowledgment of this truth through the coming of the Son of God, and also through Him to extend salvation unto all the earth. Israel was to be the nation of the Messiah in that it preserved the ideal of one God and thus prepared the world for the advent of Him who was "the only begotten Son of God."

Having taken this brief glance into the future of Abraham's seed in order to understand the purpose of God, let us now return to the actual covenant as God made it with Abram. The party of the first part in the covenant was God himself. The party of the second part was Abram and the coming seed, still not begotten when the covenant was made.

In Genesis 17 is recorded the validation of the physical covenant. Abram was now ninety-nine years old. Almost twenty-five years had elapsed since he forsook the land of the Chaldeans. Previously the Lord had appeared under the title of Jehovah. He now introduces himself as El Shaddai, God Almighty. This was assurance that whatever He promised He had the power to perform. In view of the majesty of His name, He began by instructing Abram, "Walk before me, and be thou blameless." The Lord said, "As for me, behold, my covenant is with thee, and thou shalt be a father of many nations" (Genesis 17:4; KJV). This was the fifth time God promised to make Abram the father of an innumerable progeny.

Frequently in history God memorialized an event of great significance by bestowing a new name, or by altering a previously existing one. In this instance the name of Abram was changed to Abraham. It was pointed out that "Abram" is formed by combining *ab*, father; and *ram*, chief. To this was now added *hamon*, meaning "multitude." The abbreviated form of Abramhamon, or Abraham, means "chief father of a multitude." The change in the form of address was accompanied by the words, "I will establish my covenant between me and thee and thy seed after thee in their generations for an everlasting covenant, to be a God unto thee, and to thy seed after thee" (17:7, 8; KJV). It was for this reason that Simon Peter referred to God as "the God of Abraham, and of Isaac, and of Jacob, the God of our fathers" (Acts 3:13; KJV).

Further, God promised to give to Abraham and to his seed after him the land in which he was a foreigner, or all the land of Canaan. He declared it would be an everlasting possession of his seed and further declared, "I will be their God." All covenants that God makes with man are based upon what He has done for man. It was thus enjoined upon Abraham and his posterity to keep the covenant inviolable.

"This is my covenant, which ye shall keep, between me and you and thy seed after thee; every man child among you shall be circumcised" (Genesis 17:10; KJV). The seed by which the ova is fertilized, thus causing conception, is manufactured within the body of the male. It is deposited in the body of the female through the external organ of procreation. Thus, this organ was regarded as the very instrument of life, the channel of the physical seed. It was provided that the foreskin of this organ would be clipped or cut off. This left a permanent indication of covenant relationship that was directly connected with the begetting of offspring, who were in turn to be brought into covenant relationship. The operation was to be performed when the male child was eight days old.

## A SACRED COVENANT

The Lord declared, "My covenant shall be *in your flesh* for an everlasting covenant" (v. 13). So sacred did the mark of circumcision become that when one took a solemn oath affecting future seed, he was required to place his hand on the procreative organ. This is exactly as one today may place his hand on a copy of the Holy Bible when taking a judicial or executive oath. Thus when Abraham was preparing to dispatch his faithful servant to secure a wife for Isaac, he said, "Put, I pray thee, thy hand under my thigh: and I will make thee swear by the Lord, the God of heaven, and the God of the earth, that thou shalt not take a wife unto my son of the

39

daughters of the Canaanites, among whom I dwell, but thou shalt go unto my country, and to my kindred, and take a wife unto my son Isaac" (Genesis 24:2-4; KJV).

It was furthermore declared, "And the uncircumcised man child whose flesh of his foreskin is not circumcised, that soul shall be cut off from his people; he hath broken my covenant" (17:14). It is evident that the blessings of the covenant applied to the individual, only when he had obeyed the ordinance of circumcision. The ordinance was not the covenant, but it was essential to bring one into the privileges and prerogatives of the covenant.

It was not enough simply to be born into the physical family of Abraham. If one so born was not circumcised, either through neglect or irreverence, he was cut off because he had broken the covenant.

Isaac was circumcised when he was eight days old, as God had commanded Abraham (21:4). In turn, he circumcised his own sons. Jacob, who was the father of twelve sons, did likewise with his offspring. As a result of this mark in the flesh, the nomadic tribes that descended from Abraham felt a kinship with God which was not felt by the Canaanites around them.

The writer to the Hebrews puts it in the framework of faith: "By faith Abraham, when he was called to go out into a place which he should after receive for an inheritance, obeyed; and he went out, not knowing whither he went. By faith he sojourned in the land of promise, as in a strange country, dwelling in tabernacles with Isaac and Jacob, the heirs with him of the same promise: for he looked for a city which hath foundations, whose builder and maker is God" (11:8-10; KJV).

How strange it is that these wanderers who lived in tents in the wilderness had a dream of inhabiting a city constructed by divine power. With a mark in their flesh serving as a constant reminder of the covenant, they regarded themselves as heirs of a promise spoken from Heaven. It is said of them, "These all died in faith, not having received the promises, but having seen them afar off, and were persuaded of them, and embraced them, and confessed that they were strangers and pilgrims on the earth" (Hebrews 11:13; KJV).

Perhaps those who are the seed of Abraham, whether in flesh or faith, are doomed to be always strangers and pilgrims on the earth, always looking for a city that has foundations. Perhaps there are always promises that must be seen afar off, of which we must be persuaded, and which we must embrace. But God had to create a nation on earth through which His Son could come, that the kingdom of Heaven might be received through His coming.

Chapter 4

# THE FIRST TESTAMENT

When God called Abram, it was His original intent to make of his seed a great nation. To accomplish His purpose He allowed the descendants of Abram to be cradled and conditioned in the most advanced culture of that day. Because of its fortunate situation on either side of the River Nile, Egypt had become "the breadbasket of the world." In order to transport the circumcised desert-wanderers into Egypt, divine providence employed famine, human jealousy and hostility, lies, and perfidy. It was a supreme demonstration that God can take even the vagaries and errors of humankind and direct them to the fulfillment of His ultimate design.

In Egypt the descendants of Jacob were first accorded royal treatment, but later reduced to the status of slaves. In spite of dire bondage with its hardships, the people thrived under protection from on high. The seventy souls who went down into that country with Jacob multiplied in number until they probably exceeded two million. When the proper time came, they were freed from bondage and started on the way to the land that was to be peculiarly theirs, according to promise. Without realizing it, the ruling Pharaoh had been an instrument in training the slaves to develop the very qualities essential to their attainment of nationhood. The family of the Messiah was ready to become the nation of the Messiah.

God reveals himself in a manner adapted to the state of things existing when the revelation is given. Since the cardinal purpose was to make a nation to keep alive in the minds of men the existence of one true God, it was necessary to impress upon all nations the significance of His selection of Israel as a nation separate from all others. At that time when "every nation made gods of their own" (Cp. 2 Kings 17:29), the feeling was universal that the power of a god could be determined by two factors. One was the state of the people over whose fate he was alleged to preside, and the other was the works of wonder performed in their behalf. If a nation prospered materially, was strong in battle, and triumphed over others, it was conceded that the god of such a nation was a powerful deity.

To gain a proper degree of respect and reverence for himself and the chosen people, God accepted this criterion and proceeded to demonstrate His superiority. Since His people were slaves in Egypt, the

43

first manifestation of power was against that nation and its gods. He selected as an ambassador one who had been reared and educated in the king's palace, but who had become a political exile under charge of homicide. God sent him to the royal court with a positive ultimatium to the Pharaoh to let His people go. When the haughty monarch denied any knowledge of the God of Israel, it became necessary for God to show His divinity. To be effective to mankind, any proof divine power must be supernatural and capable of being fully perceived.

Ten different demonstrations were manifested in Egypt. The first three were simply to prove that Jehovah was the Lord. "And the Egyptians shall know that I am the Lord, when I stretch forth my hand upon Egypt" (Exodus 7:5; KJV). The next three were to demonstrate that He was also God in Egypt and that the deities of the land were impotent before Him. To this end He drew a line of demarcation between Goshen, the province where Israel dwelt, and the rest of Egypt. "I will sever in that day the land of Goshen, in which my people dwell, that no swarms of flies shall be there; to the end thou mayest know that I am the Lord in the midst of the earth. And I will put a division between my people and thy people: to morrow shall this sign be" (Exodus 8:22, 23; KJV). Goshen was unaffected by the succeeding disasters that paralyzed the remainder of the country.

The third series of three catastrophic events advanced one more step. They proved that there was none like Him in all the earth. " 'This time I will send all my plagues upon your heart, and upon your servants and your people, that you may know there is none like me in all the earth. For by now I could have put forth my hand and struck you and your people with pestilence, and you would have been cut off from the earth; but for this purpose have I let you live, to show you my power, so that my name may be declared throughout all the earth.' " (Exodus 9:14-16; RSV).

At the very birth of the nation, the final blow to Egypt was destined to prove that this God was a master of all gods. He proposed to deliver these bondslaves without revolt, clash of arms, or loss of a single life among them. At this time Egypt was the mightiest nation on earth. The Pharaoh was feared above every other earthly monarch. On the night appointed for Israel's deliverance, the slaves demanded of their masters jewelry of silver and gold. God moved upon the hearts of the Egyptians to grant this request. Another factor entering into the transaction was the reputation that Moses had gained in the eyes of the Egyptians, by reason of the mighty works done through him (Exodus 11:3).

At midnight the death angel passed through the land with terrible execution. He smote all of the firstborn, "from the firstborn of Pharaoh that sat on his throne unto the firstborn of the captive that was in the dungeon; and all the firstborn of cattle" (Exodus 12:29; KJV). Yet, "against any of the people of Israel shall not a dog move his tongue" (11:7). There was a great cry of anguish in Egypt, for there was not a house in which there was not one dead. The agonized Pharaoh did not wait until morning. He summoned Moses and Aaron by night and said, "Rise up, and get you forth from among my people, both ye and the children of Israel; and go, serve the Lord, as ye have said. Also take your flocks and your herds, as ye have said, and be gone; and bless me also" (12:31, 32).

When the full realization of what he had done dawned upon the Pharaoh, he changed his mind, and decided to pursue the Israelites and return them to slavery. The Israelites trembled when they saw the approaching Egyptians, but Moses said, " 'Fear not, stand firm, and see the salvation of the Lord, which he will work for you today; for the Egyptians whom you see today, you shall never see again. The Lord will fight for you, and you have only to be still' " (Exodus 14:13, 14; RSV). Lifting his rod over the waters of the Red Sea, he caused them to part by the power of God.

The people of Israel marched through the sea on dry ground, and the Egyptian cavalry, attempting to follow, were all drowned.

So mighty was this feat that many years later Moses asked, " 'Has any god ever attempted to go and take a nation for himself from the midst of another nation, by trials, by signs, by wonders, and by war, by a mighty hand and an outstretched arm, and by great terrors, according to all that the Lord your God did for you in Egypt before your eyes? To you it was shown, that you might know that the Lord is God; there is no other besides him' " (Deuteronomy 4:34, 35; RSV). The expression, "take a nation for himself," is a key phrase in any study of the relationship of God to Israel. In fulfilling His design God showed His superiority to the gods of the most prosperous and flourishing nation of the day.

## THE NATIONAL CONSTITUTION

It is one thing to lead a group of slaves from the land of bondage, and a wholly different matter to weld them into a nation. To accomplish the latter, the first thing required is some system of laws or a constitution, by which the people shall be governed. In a theocracy such a constitution would have to be in the nature of an announced covenant. Accordingly, after God had freed the people of Israel, He did not allow them to take the direct route to Canaan, which would have led them by the way of the Philistine garrisons. Instead, God turned them southward toward Mount Sinai, and around the base of this peak they established their camp. Here God made known His intention to submit to the people *en masse* the question of whether or not they would be willing to enter into the covenant relationship with Him, accepting such responsibility as would be entailed. Thus, the Creator preserved the dignity and respected the will of creatures made in His own image, although He was under no obligation to deal with them on this exalted level.

Moses, the mediator, was summoned to come up into the mountain, and he ascended in the presence of all the people. The proposal of God was committed to Moses to convey to the entire multitude. It was conditioned upon the one great act of deliverance in which the Egyptians had suffered frightful retribution and Israel had been miraculously reclaimed. Moses was told, " 'Thus you shall say to the house of Jacob, and tell the people of Israel: You have seen what I did to the Egyptians, and how I bore you on eagles' wings and brought you to myself' " (Exodus 19:3, 4; RSV). This was deemed of sufficient power to make Israel recognize an indebtedness to God and to inspire them to trust in His might for the future. With them, nationhood began, not in a resolution of human determination, but in a mighty act of God. For that reason the proposal was made, " 'Now therefore, if you will obey my voice and keep my covenant, you shall be my own possession among all peoples; for all the earth is mine, and you shall be to me a kingdom of priests and a holy nation. These are the words which you shall speak to the children of Israel' " (vv. 5, 6; RSV).

Since there was no central means of communication available, and no mass media through which one person might speak to more than two million persons, Moses summoned the elders and relayed to them the message of God. He asked them to ascertain the will of the people and report back to him the results of their poll. The people unanimously agreed, saying, " 'All that the Lord has spoken we will do' " (v. 8). Moses reported their decision to God, who informed him that He would personally address the people on the third day in a manner that they could not forget. As a preliminary for the occasion, the mountain was to be regarded as sacred. A boundary line must be drawn, across which the people were not to set foot. The death sentence was decreed for any man or animal crossing the line. During the interval the people were to wash their garments and abstain from all sexual relations. The blast of a heavenly trumpet would signal the beginning of the announcement of the covenant.

On the morning of the third day there were thunders and lightnings. A thick cloud dropped down to enshroud the mountain. A loud trumpet blast echoed among the peaks. Sinai was enveloped in smoke, and the entire mountain shook and trembled. The startled people were brought forth to stand and gaze at the awesome spectacle while wondering what the future held for them. Moses spoke, and God answered in the rumbling of thunder.

Moses never forgot the inaugural ceremony for the covenant. Shortly before his death he addressed the people in these words, " 'For ask now of the days that are past, which were before you, since the day that God created man upon the earth, and ask from one end of heaven to the other, whether such a great thing as this has ever happened or was ever heard of. Did any people ever hear the voice of a god speaking out of the midst of the fire, as you have heard, and still live? Out of heaven he let you hear his voice, that he might discipline you; and on earth he let you see his great fire, and you heard his words out of the midst of the fire' " (Deuteronomy 4:32, 33; 36; RSV).

Chapter 5

# ANALYSIS OF THE COVENANT

The eager student of God's revelation should have an overwhelming desire, an unquenchable passion, to ascertain the truth. He should not be deterred in his search for this "golden fleece" by his own past conclusions or by present popular error. This is said because of certain statements that will be made. Though based upon Scriptural testimony, these will challenge a view so deeply entrenched that even to question it will appear like heresy. Yet, it is not too much to say that our whole personal relationship to God may be directly affected by what is written in the remainder of this volume.

All of us realize that the words "testament" and "covenant" are used interchangeably in the Authorized Version. Thus the apostle Paul speaks of "the reading of the old testament" in 2 Corinthians 3:14, and the writer of Hebrews calls it a "covenant" in Hebrews 8:9. The original word is the same in both instances. In your copy of the sacred Scriptures, the title page probably bears this statement: "The Holy

51

Bible, containing the Old and New Testaments." This statement is correct, but not in the sense it is intended. There are not thirty-nine books in "the old testament." There are not twenty-seven books in the "new testament." In fact, the new covenant, or new testament, was never written with pen and ink at all. The record given by the Spirit states this very clearly.

Because men have labeled the thirty-nine books constituting the Jewish Scriptures the "Old Testament," virtually the whole world has been led to believe that this entire compilation constituted the covenant with God. No idea could be more incorrect. None is fraught with greater possibility for error in understanding the unfolding of God's purpose. Laboring under this delusion, many people have completely missed the purpose of God, which is conveyed in "the new covenant." They have merely substituted one legalistic written code for another as the basis of their service to God and communion with one another.

Any understanding of the "new covenant" must be attained through a proper concept of the old. If the second is not to be like the first, a correct survey of the first will prepare for a rational investigation of the second. What was the nature of the "old covenant"? Why was it given? What did it embrace? What were its bounds and limitations? A proper evaluation of these matters will make it possible for us to place "the Jacob's staff" of our spiritual survey at the exact spot from which to look at the "better covenant, which was established upon better promises" (8:6; KJV).

Let us remember that nowhere in all the sacred writings does God ever suggest that all of the Holy Scriptures from Moses to Malachi constitute "the old testament," or covenant. No inspired writer ever hinted that the "old testament" contains thirty-nine books. Some of these books recount the history and chronicles of the covenant people. One is a collection of songs and psalms used in the praise service of the covenant people. Some contain the literature and proverbs collected by the covenant people. Many are prophetic warnings and promises made to people of the covenant. But the history of such a covenant people is no more a part of their constitution than a book on American history is part of the Constitution of the United States. Such a history may refer to our Constitution, detail our departures from its principles, and urge our return to its original spirit, but it is not the Constitution or our national covenant.

A nation is a social unit, created when a number of clans or tribes associate themselves together for mutual progress and protection. In the very nature of things, the first requirement is a compact, or agreement. Such an agreement is called a covenant, or constitution. When God calls a nation out for himself, it is evident that such a nation must constitute a theocracy. Being such and not a democracy, God must announce the terms of the relationship involved.

The preamble of the constitution was a proclamation of what God had done for them. God never enjoins a covenant upon the human family except upon the basis of prior deeds in their behalf. In this instance, the preface would serve for all ages to identify the people involved and the God whom they were to serve. In solemn tones, the words were uttered, " 'I am the Lord your God, who brought you out of the land of Egypt, out of the house of bondage' " (Exodus 20:2; RSV). The covenant was made possible by a divine act of deliverance. Freedom was accorded by what God did for them, not by what they did for God.

There followed Ten Commandments, which with the preamble constituted what the inspired writers call "the old covenant" or "the first testament." Since a nation is a social unit, its people sustain a dual relationship—to God and one another. The Ten Commandments are divided into two classes, the first four pertaining to man's responsibility to God; the last six to man's responsibility to man.

54

# PERTAINING TO GOD

The initial Commandment was the keystone in the arch of national purpose. It struck at the very heart of polytheism, and forever made monotheism the foundation of covenant relationship on the part of Israel. " 'You shall have no other gods before me' " (Exodus 20:3; RSV). This made the worship of idols an act of treason, a revolt against the sovereign power, and an overt manifestation of conspiracy to overthrow the nation by subverting it from its original purpose and intent. By statute it was made a capital offense.

The second and third statements were made against treasonable intent. Knowing the tendency of man to worship what he creates, it was forbidden to make any graven image or the likeness of any creature in the universe. To bow down before the work of the sculptor or graver, or to give any homage thereto, was also a capital offense. The third Commandment was designed to forbid any lessening of respect or awe for the name of Jehovah. " 'You shall not take the name of the Lord your God in vain' " (v. 7; RSV). To "take the name of the Lord" was to call upon God to witness a promise or vow. This was generally done by saying, "As the Lord liveth I will do this or that." To do so in vain meant to take such an oath in the name of God without any intention of fulfilling it. "Men indeed swear by a greater than themselves, and in all their disputes an oath is final for confirmation" (Hebrews 6:16; RSV). Since this was the final appeal for confirmation, reverence for the name of God would soon disappear if He were called upon to sanction a falsehood or empty promise.

The fourth Commandment stipulated the percentage of time to be accorded the Lawgiver and King. One day in seven was to be assigned to Him in honor of two great events. His creative work ended, and He rested on the seventh day. On the same day He brought the people out of Egypt. By hallowing the seventh day they would be commemorating the creation of the earth and the creation of a nation to honor the God of the universe. The method of consecration was the same that God himself originally employed: rest, or relaxation, and absolute cessation from creativity.


## PERTAINING TO OTHERS

Before we mention the fifth Commandment, a few words are in order about the method of perpetuating the knowledge of the covenant. There was no provision made for propagandizing people of other nations. No recruiting program was inaugurated. If one who dwelt among the people desired to enroll with them, he could do so by allowing himself and other males in the family to be circumcised. This was voluntary. There was no solicitation for him to do so. It is true that after they had been scattered among all nations, the descendants of Abraham, having burdened their law with cumbersome traditions, enlisted Gentiles whom they transformed into fanatical zealots worse than themselves, but this was not the original intent.

Carrying forward the patriarchal procedure, the fathers were directly charged with the responsibility of instructing their children. The solemn duty was enjoined immediately following the *Shema*, the watchword of Israel. After pronouncing it Moses said, "And these words, which I command thee this day, shall be in thine heart: and thou shalt teach them diligently unto thy children, and shalt talk to them when thou sittest in thine house, and when thou walkest by the way, and when thou liest down, and when thou risest up" (Deuteronomy 6:6, 7; KJV). Each home was to be a school upon whose gates and doorposts these things were written.

This implies that the Torah, as Israel used the term to designate the "Law of Moses," was simple enough in essence for the fathers to expound and for the children to understand. It was only when professional teachers arose and eventually divided into representatives and defenders of various schools of thought that the word became obscured by vain janglings. Inasmuch as the parents were ordained as the sacred teachers, it is not surprising that the next Commandment, following those relating to the proper attitude toward God, enjoined reverence for them. "Honour thy father and thy mother" (Exodus 20:12; KJV). The parent stood in the room of God to the offspring, giving them the Torah as God gave it to mankind originally.

The remainder of the Ten Commandments constituted the great moral or ethical code intended to set the people apart from the degenerate worshipers of other gods. Taken together they compose "the old testament" or covenant. All other laws, statutes, and judgments, grew out of a relationship to these. While other laws carried a penalty for violation, the national existence was not necessarily impaired or destroyed by disregard for them. But the Ten Commandments constituted the national covenant, the constitution. Upon this covenant the nation had been formed, and by that covenant it would continue to exist. A disregard for the covenant would bring about the dissolution of national sovereignty, unless the breach was repaired firmly and decisively.

The books of history, poetry, and prophecy, are not part of the covenant.

They are Scriptures, or writings, which grew out of the relationship created by the covenant, but they are not "the first testament," as God employs that term. That which established covenant relationship and created the nation was one thing. The sacred books written to the covenant people, or nationals, constituted a wholly different thing. Because we have familiarly and thoughtlessly spoken of the thirty-nine books as composing "the old testament" and have subscribed to this popular error, it is necessary to re-examine the Scriptures related to this matter.

But one may ask what difference it makes. This is the refuge of those who would rather continue in error than discover truth. We have already established that God's entire relationship with man has been revealed as being on a covenantal basis. Does it make a difference whether we have a correct or an incorrect view of what constitutes a covenant of God? Can any professed follower of our Lord be respected who ridicules, derides, or scoffs at a matter so grave that it strikes at the very root of our approach to Deity? Is one deserving of reverence as an instructor in holy things who deliberately chooses to ignore truth and continues to teach error? Such may be worthy of those who would place a sect above all else. Surely it has no place in the life or thought of men and women who love the truth more than life itself.

There is an even more serious and sobering aspect. The covenantal relationship of old was a school of instruction for those who live under "the new covenant." If we mistake the nature of the "old covenant," its scope and breadth, we can as easily be wrong about the new. If this happens, we may ignore the ongoing purpose of God and merely substitute one system of legality for another as the ground of justification. By doing this we will again bind a yoke upon men "which neither our fathers nor we were able to bear" (Acts 15:10; KJV).

It is easy to develop a pharisaical attitude about the New Covenant Scriptures as about the Old. If we condition our relationship with God on the basis of knowing a compilation of sacred writings, rather than faith in Jesus, we actually make the Bible our God. As a result, we become inconsistent and insecure. Every interpretation, exegesis, or opinion that disagrees with our own is considered treason. Our problem is that we make the basis of our hope an agreement with men, not a covenant with God. One may be wrong about many things who is in a covenant relationship, but the covenant is not broken by his error. God's covenants are made with a variety of men. They do not all think alike, nor can they all do so.

Chapter 6

# THE COVENANT OF LAW

The terms "old testament" and "old covenant" are used interchangeably in the sacred Scriptures. The "old covenant" was written upon two tablets of stone. On the basis of that covenant the chosen people had been called out of slavery to constitute a nation. Nothing that had been said prior to the giving of the two stone tablets was a part of the covenant. Nothing that was written subsequently was a part of it. Certainly all that God had said before and all He said afterward sustained a relationship to the covenant, but the covenant itself was a distinct instrument. Of this, Moses is our first and best witness, for he received the original draft of the constitution.

Thirty-eight years later, in the plains of Moab, Moses rehearsed in the ears of the surviving children of the original covenantees, a summary of the things that transpired: "And ye came near and stood under the mountain; and the mountain burned with fire unto the midst of heaven, with darkness, clouds, and thick darkness. And the Lord spake unto you out of the midst of the fire: ye heard the voice of the words, but saw no similitude; only ye heard a voice. And he declared unto you his covenant, which he commanded you to perform, even ten commandments; and he wrote them upon two tables of stone" (Deuteronomy 4:11-13; KJV).

More explicit yet is the account in Deuteronomy 5: "The Lord our God made a covenant with us in Horeb. The Lord made not this covenant with our fathers, but with us, even us, who are all of us here alive this day" (vv. 2, 3). Certainly, then, the first sixty-nine chapters of the Bible are not a part of "the first covenant" mentioned in Hebrews 8:7, for they deal with the fathers previous to the encounter at Sinai, and the Lord did not make the covenant with the fathers.

Just as Moses eliminates from the covenant the sacred writings dealing with prior history, he also eliminates all future writings from it. He repeats the Ten Commandments as the covenant, then concludes: "These words the Lord spake unto all your assembly in the mount out of the midst of the fire, of the cloud, and of the thick darkness, with a great voice: *and he added no more.* And he wrote them in two tables of stone, and delivered them to me" (v. 22). Although God "added no more," men have added some thirty-seven books of history, chronicles, poetry, songs, wise sayings, prophecies, and apocalyptic writings to the covenant made at Horeb. When they speak of "the old testament," they include all of these in their concept.

Even worse than this, they carry that same concept over to "the new covenant." They make our very relationship to God and one another dependent upon their idea, denying that anyone who disagrees with their theological slant can be in covenant with God. This defeats the very purpose of God and negates the reconciliation effected by the cross. If God deals with us as a covenant-making God, and men confuse the covenant with writings addressed to the covenant people, our relationship is not conditioned upon faith but upon our intellectual apprehension of abstract matters.

We respectfully submit that a consideration of the following points will help all of us to realize that "the first testament" did not include all of the Scriptures now called the Old Testament.

1. The two tables of stone are distinctly said to be the tables of the covenant (Deuteronomy 9:11). They are called the "tables of stone, even the tables of the covenant" (v. 9).

2. The sacred chest, or coffer, containing the tablets of stone was called "the ark of the covenant" (Numbers 10:33; Deuteronomy 10:8). When Solomon erected the

temple, he said, "In it have I put the ark, wherein is the covenant of the Lord, that he made with the children of Israel" (2 Chronicles 6:11). The ark had disappeared before many of the books of prophecy were even written. Not one of the books of prophecy was ever in the ark, because not one was a part of the covenant.

3. The covenant was distinctly said to have been made and given in Horeb (Deuteronomy 5:2). The apostle Paul identified this as Mount Sinai in Arabia (Galatians 4:24, 25). But most of the rest of the Old Covenant Scriptures were written in Palestine, Babylon, or Persia.

4. The covenant was said to have been made when God "took them by the hand to bring them out of the land of Egypt" (Jeremiah 31:32). The Scriptures were written much later and in many other places.

5. Certainly the prophecy of Jeremiah was no part of the "first testament," for by the time Jeremiah wrote, the people had already broken the covenant of God. The prophet predicted that a new covenant would be made (Jeremiah 31:31).

The words of "the old testament" which God made with Israel were first announced orally by the voice of God. These words embraced the Ten Commandments and the preamble that identified God. The finger of God then wrote the words upon two stone tablets (Deuteronomy 9:10). The covenant

64

was limited to the content of the oral message that was subsequently engraved upon the two tablets, for *the Lord added no more.*

When the people had heard the words of God, they were so frightened that the heads of the tribes approached Moses and besought him, "Go thou near, and hear all that the Lord our God shall say: and speak thou unto us all that the Lord our God shall speak unto thee; and we will hear it, and do it" (Deuteronomy 5:27; KJV). The Lord agreed to this arrangement. He instructed Moses to go and tell the people to return to their tents. However, He told Moses, "Stand thou here by me, and I will speak unto thee all the commandments, and the statutes, and the judgments, which thou shalt teach them" (v. 31). There was a difference between the covenant and the various statutes, commands, and ordinances. The covenant established the nation's relationship as the elect of God, and the other commands regulated the people within that relationship. The apostle Paul recognized this distinction when he wrote, "They are Israelites, and to them belong the sonship, the glory, the covenants, the giving of the law, the worship, and the promises" (Romans 9:4; RSV).

The covenant made at Sinai, through which national theocratic status was conferred upon Israel, was of such a nature as to require a definite written code to accomplish its design. The law is personified as a "child-conductor" or "custodian" (Galatians 3:24; RSV). It was a guardian or trustee (Galatians 4:2; RSV). Those who were under its jurisdiction were regarded as children, or minors, thus possessing no more freedom than slaves (Galatians 4:1). Now, just as no one would entrust a child to the care of another who was immature, so the nation at its inception required a law that was complete. A foundation is not constructed gradually, after a structure has been erected. A nation founded upon law must have the law to produce the nation. Accordingly, the Lord revealed to the original mediator the law in its fullness.

The first covenant was a legalistic arrangement. It was designed to keep its subjects in confinement and under restraint, and so the covenant itself was legalistic. It consisted of law. The covenant given through Moses was law, but not all the laws given through Moses were part of the covenant. This will explain such statements as that of Paul, "I had not known sin, but by the law: for I had not known lust, except the law had said, Thou shalt not covet" (Romans 7:7; KJV). This statement is a part of the covenant. It is one of the Ten Commandments. But the covenant was the groundwork of a legal system. Because of this, other portions of the Scriptures which grew out of this legal covenant are referred to as "law." They are parts of a legal system.

It is important that we understand the nature of a system of law as opposed to a system of faith for justification before God. If we fail to do so, we may simply substitute one law for another, and this would be a fatal error. Any person who seeks to be justified by law must keep that law to perfection. If one proposes to establish a relationship based upon deeds of law, he must maintain a meticulous and unvarying obedience to every command, regardless of how minute it may seem. His very life will depend upon such obedience, for he is trading his deeds for life. "The law does not rest on faith, for 'He who does them shall live by them'" (Galatians 3:12; RSV). To put that in reverse, it simply teaches that a man can live under the law only if he does absolutely everything the law requires. The slightest deviation brings condemnation and death.

One cannot set up in his heart a system of justification by law, and then expect God's grace to rescue him in his failures. Grace operates through faith and not by law. If we are now under any kind of a written code, seeking for justification, our only hope (if hope it may be called) is to live in constant fear and dread, and keep every provision of that written code without fail.

This being true, the question naturally

arises, "Why then the law?" Why did God institute a covenant consisting of a written code? The question is not new. It was first propounded by an avid student of the law in Galatians 3:19. The inspired answer is found at the same place: "It was added because of transgressions, till the offspring should come to whom the promise had been made" (RSV). The "offspring" is identified in the context as Jesus Christ. The law was added to the promise made to Abraham, and was intended to act as a custodian to guard and guide the people in their immaturity until they could be brought to Christ.

But justification did not come by the law, "for if justification were through the law, then Christ died to no purpose" (Galatians 2:21; RSV). It is plainly said, "by works of the law shall no one be justified" (2:16; RSV). Again, "It is evident that no man is justified before God by the law" (3:11). No written code can ever produce life. The law in its ultimate could produce only death. Since justification by law demands absolute conformity to the minutest degree, and since no man could fulfill the law's demand to this extent, "The very commandment which promised life proved to be death to me" (Romans 7:10; RSV); "For if a law had been given which could make alive, then righteousness would indeed be by the law" (Galatians 3:21).

# Chapter 7

# WEAKNESS OF THE LAW

We must not fall into the error of thinking that the law given to and by Moses had built-in imperfections because of its origin or agency of transmission. It originated with God, and Moses was such an outstanding person that God said He spoke to him "face to face, as a man speaks to his friend." The perfect God did not give an imperfect law. The law was perfectly adapted to the purpose for which it was intended. Its inability to justify lay in the fact that it was *a law*, a written code, not that it was the law of God.

So long as man is in the flesh, in his human nature, he cannot be justified by such a written code, regardless of its origin. The weakness is not in the code but in the flesh. Just as law places restraints on what man is allowed to do in the flesh, so the nature of man places restrictions on what the law is able to accomplish. There are things that law cannot do with us because we are in the flesh.

The law given by Moses was of divine origin. It was not unholy or unjust, for "It

69

was ordained by angels through an intermediary" (Galatians 3:19; RSV). It was not an unspiritual arrangement, for "we know that the law is spiritual" (Romans 7:14; RSV). We can only conclude, "The law is holy, and the commandment holy, and just, and good" (Romans 7:12). How could that which came from God, was furnished by angels, was holy, just, good, and spiritual, fail to produce life? The answer is that its failure is not in its source or character. It failed simply because man is what he is. The very essence of man's justification by law is absolute and unvarying conformity. This requires man's perfect knowledge and understanding from the very moment he comes under the law. If he makes one mistake he becomes guilty under the law, and all of his good deeds in the future can never purge that guilt. Man is incapable of such perfection.

*The law cannot justify*, because it arouses carnal desires or passions. We must deal with man as he is. Filled with curiosity, the urge to experiment, and the ambition to learn by experience, man is lured to destruction by that which is forbidden. The very commandment intended to restrain all too often incites. The law identifies sin, points it out, and locates it as surely as a "Wet Paint" sign on a park bench warns the passerby. The apostle says, "If it had not been for the law, I should not have known sin. I should not have known what it is to covet if the law had not said, 'You shall not covet.' But sin, *finding opportunity in the commandment*, wrought in me all kinds of covetousness" (Romans 7:7, 8; RSV). The tragic feature is that the penalty is death. There is no mercy in law, only justice! "For sin, finding opportunity in the commandment, deceived me and *by it killed me*" (7:11; RSV). This is the inexorable fate of the legalist, one who seeks to be justified by law. He cannot escape it. His own testimony as to his imperfection will condemn him.

*The law could not give life.* It is not within the province of any written code to do so. But the law could and did bring knowledge of sin. "For no human being will be justified in his sight by works of the law, since through the law comes knowledge of sin" (3:20; RSV). The plain force of this passage is that the greater one's knowledge of law, the more he realizes his own sinfulness and human weakness. The word "law" has many shades of meaning in the sacred Scriptures. Ignorance of this leads to some absurd and false conclusions. The strict and proper meaning is "a rule of conduct, prescribed by superior authority." In the final analysis, the character of the authority determines the objective of the law. God is holy, and He desires that we be holy. His nature is the criterion for our measurement. When we apply the law to our conduct, we are made to see our own failures and shortcomings. The more we learn of the law the greater becomes our sense of guilt and inadequacy.

*The law could and did bring wrath:* "For the law brings wrath, but where there is no law there is no transgression" (4:15; RSV). The law provided for the conscience a standard external to itself. If there were no law, there would be no sense of transgression and no guilt. With a code of laws before him, man can determine the utter futility of trying to become perfect by law-keeping, and thus be led to see the need of a Savior.

*The law made nothing complete, or perfect.* In that respect it was weak and useless. This is affirmed by the writer to the Hebrews: "On the one hand, a former commandment is set aside because of its weakness and uselessness (for the law made nothing perfect)" (Hebrews 7:18, 19; RSV). But this did not militate against the law in fulfilling its assigned role. Its purpose was to hold man in restraint until Christ came. Justification was not to be found in the law, but in the love that manifested itself in the Son of God.

The covenant, which bound Israel to the true and living God in a relationship of intimacy that was comparable to marriage, was repeatedly violated by the nation. That constant violation demonstrated that

72

a covenant consisting of a written code could never make man guiltless before God. For this reason, Jeremiah, the priestly prophet, predicted the advent of a new covenant, which would be of a different nature. Written codes are external, but the new covenant was to be internal. It was not to be written upon stone tablets or papyrus sheets, but upon human hearts.

"Behold, the days come, saith the Lord, that I will make a new covenant with the house of Israel, and with the house of Judah: not according to the covenant that I made with their fathers in the day that I took them by the hand to bring them out of the land of Egypt; which my covenant they brake, although I was an husband unto them, saith the Lord: but this shall be the covenant that I will make with the house of Israel; After those days, saith the Lord, I will put my law in their inward parts, and write it in their hearts; and will be their God, and they shall be my people. And they shall teach no more every man his neighbour, and every man his brother, saying, Know the Lord: for they shall all know me, from the least of them unto the greatest of them, saith the Lord: for I will forgive their iniquity, and I will remember their sin no more" (Jeremiah 31:31-34; KJV).

As a prelude to our discussion of that new covenant which God has made with us in Christ, let us consider an analysis of this prophetic promise.

The covenant to come was to be a *new* one. It was not to be an extension of the old, nor was it to be a renewed application or imposition of the terms of any previous agreement. The first covenant was made when the fathers were delivered from slavery in Egypt; the new one would be made when men were delivered from the bondage of sin. The new covenant would be unlike the former one. The former covenant was the constitution for a physical nation upon earth; the second was for a spiritual kingdom made up of those called out from every nation upon the earth.

The legal code ordained at Horeb did not succeed in binding the people to God. Instead, they lived by their lusts and trusted in the fact that they had the law in their possession. They worshiped the tables of the covenant and the ark in which they were contained. In time of battle they carried it to the field of conflict, exactly as other nations bore their images of worship and in which they trusted for victory. The nation broke the covenant, even though God was faithful as a husband. The nation chose other gods, but God chose no other nation.

The new covenant was not to be a written code. Its sanctuary was not to be the room behind the second veil of an earthly temple, but the inner being of a consecrated person. God placed the tablets of stone in the Holy of Holies under the Shekinah, the glory of His presence. Now His law, His principle of action, is not enshrined in a book but within the spirit of man. The body is the temple of God. The inner man is the holy of holies. Here God's glory is seen and experienced through the indwelling Spirit. Once God put His law in a sacred chest created by men. Now His love, as a divine law, is enshrined in a spiritual treasure-house of His own creation. He said, "I will put my law in their inward parts." The covenant is not chiseled in stone. It is not written upon paper. It is not printed but imprinted. It is engraved on the heart.

The new covenant is individual in nature. It is secure in the inner being, that is, in the heart of the faithful person. One does not belong to God because he belongs to a covenant people. He belongs to the covenant people because he belongs to God. He does not arrive at a covenantal status by subscribing to a code, but by surrender to the Christ. God is the God of those who have bared the walls of their hearts to the inscription written by the finger of God. Those who have covenanted with Him are His people. Any person upon this earth who has entered into the covenantal relationship with God is a child of God, and that covenant pledges his allegiance to God. So long as life continues he must have no other gods.

The old covenant, based upon the flesh of Abraham, was entered at birth. It was ratified on the eighth day of the life of the male child, by circumcision, a cutting of his flesh. The child knew nothing about the covenant. He did not know God. He was first introduced into the covenant and then taught to know the Lord. The new covenant was to be different. It was not to be based upon the flesh, but upon the spirit. It was to be the result of a personal choice, an individual acceptance of God. It would not be necessary to teach those under the new covenant to know God, for they had to know Him to be in the covenant.

There is nothing in Jeremiah's prophecy to suggest or intimate that brothers and neighbors would not teach each other under the new covenant how to live a life above reproach. It is simply that they will not need to teach those in the covenant to know the Lord. The promise is that all who are in the new relationship will have had their iniquity forgiven. God will remember their transgressions no more.

We have come to the place in the study to give attention to the new and different covenant. We have the assurance that it is "a better covenant, which was established upon better promises" (Hebrews 8:6; KJV).

# Chapter 8

# THE TIME OF REFORMATION

In a wonderful treatise contained in three chapters of Hebrews (8, 9, 10), the writer summarizes what he had previously written about the superiority of the new covenant over the old. He begins the section with the words, "Now of the things which we have spoken this is the sum" (KJV). Twice in this limited framework he refers to the promise of God through Jeremiah, that He intended to make "a new covenant" (8:8-12; 10:15-17). Of special significance is the catalog of observances and ordinances under the "old covenant," which were "imposed on them until the time of reformation" (9:10).

The next four words are, "But Christ being come." The covenant of law was temporary and transitory. It was to exist only until the time for the great change had come. It was a time of reformation, which was to be ushered in by the coming of Christ. He was to be "the mediator of a better covenant, which was established upon better promises" (8:6). It is this "better covenant" which creates and cements our relationship to God, and we should turn our attention to God's revelation concerning it with a great deal of eagerness.

The advent of Jesus to the earth constituted the watershed of human history. Jesus is the "Great Divide." He is the "new covenant," the Word of God, which became flesh and "dwelt among us, . . . full of grace and truth." All who receive Him receive of the fullness that is in Him. They become partakers of grace and truth. "For the law was given by Moses, but grace and truth came by Jesus Christ" (John 1:17; KJV).

The casual reader may overlook the profound significance of this statement. The law was *given* by Moses. The medium was not the message. Moses was not the law. The law was external to Moses. It was even written by another and handed to him. The law outlived Moses. It survived his death. But grace and truth *came* by Jesus Christ. They were not given by Him as the law was given by Moses. He was full of grace and truth. When Jesus came, grace and truth came. These constituted His "fullness," His nature, His essence.

Law is always external. It is always imposed from outside. It can never make man good. It can only make him wish he had been good. The coming of Jesus brought an end to law as a basis of anyone's relationship to God. Law, as a written code, was suspended and superseded by grace and truth. We are no longer governed by a written code. We are not under law, but under grace.

Jesus did not simply eliminate the law of Moses as a futile manner of attempting to secure righteousness. He did away with the "law principle." He did not substitute one written code for another. Instead of giving us a law, He gave himself. It is not by trust in deeds of law, but by faith in Him as a person that we secure and sustain a right relationship with the Father. Law has gone and faith has come. Moses stands in history as the giver of law. Jesus stands in history as the giver of life!

Law confines, restricts, and inhibits. It is a police power that keeps man down by keeping him under. It is a prison compound in which man is shut up. It is a custodian charged with guarding him and delivering him safely to his destination. No man is free under law. Law and liberty are antithetical to one another. The role of law is described in poignant terms in Galatians 3:23-26. Obviously, Paul is here speaking of the law given by Moses, the law that was announced 430 years after the covenant made with Abraham (3:17). But what he has to say will apply to any written code, as we shall see.

Paul uses the expressions "before faith came" (v. 23) and "after that faith is come" (v. 25). The period "before faith came" is identified as the time when men were kept under the law. The word "kept" means guarded, or under surveillance, as by *keepers of a prison*. Certainly there were men of faith under the law, but there is a difference between men coming to faith, and faith coming to men. The first is a personal trust in God. The last is a principle of justification in Christ, which came as a historical event. That faith had not come while man was under a written code. He was "shut up unto the faith which should afterwards be revealed" (v. 23).

If the law was helpless to justify, or make men righteous, what was its function? The answer is simple. "Wherefore the law was our schoolmaster to bring us unto Christ, that we might be justified by faith" (v. 24). Unfortunately, this rendering in the *King James Version* can be misleading because of the meaning we attach to "schoolmaster." We think of such a person as a teacher in school, but that is not the meaning of the original at all.

The word *paidagogos* was applied to a trusted slave who was made the guardian of a boy and charged with his upbringing. When a lad in a Roman or Greek household reached a certain age he was consigned to the keeping of such a slave. That slave was expected to control and direct the boy's life, regulate his conduct, and supervise his behavior until he reached the age of puberty.

The word literally means a "child-conductor." Our best English equivalent is "custodian."

The law was like a custodian, to guard and guide God's people until they were safely delivered to Jesus, so they could be justified by faith in Him. After faith came we "are no longer under a custodian." If we are under another written code, we are under a custodian. If we make the New Covenant Scriptures a code of laws, we constitute them a custodian. It is one of those very Scriptures which here declares that we are no longer under a custodian. We are not in custody, we are in Christ. The custodian is dead.

If our covenantal relationship with God is not established on the basis of a legal code, what is its nature? Fortunately we are not left in ignorance on this important matter. In 2 Corinthians 3, the apostle Paul describes the two covenants and graphically portrays the difference between them. Every person who is interested in establishing a right relationship with God should pay special attention to what is here revealed. That this is a contrast between the two covenants is evident. In the sixth verse Paul speaks of "the new testament." In the fourteenth verse he speaks of "the old testament."

The chapter begins with two questions. These were probably provoked by false

81

apostles at Corinth who resented Paul and questioned the validity of his apostleship. "Do we begin again to commend ourselves? or need we, as some others, epistles of commendation to you, or letters of commendation from you?" At the time when the apostle asked this question, letters of introduction, recommendation, and approval were common. Travel was widespread, and those who went from place to place carried documents that were signed by well-known political and business figures. These documents served to make the traveler's way easier when going into other countries.

There is every reason to believe that the primitive saints adopted the practice, writing letters of commendation which made it possible for the bearer to be received without question. Such a letter was sent by the congregation at Jerusalem regarding Judas and Silas (Acts 15:22-31). When Apollos prepared to go from Ephesus to Greece, "the brethren wrote, exhorting the disciples to receive him" (Acts 18:27). The letter to Philemon was such a letter.

There was nothing wrong with letters of commendation, but the apostle did not need such a letter to Corinth from other congregations, nor did he require a letter from them to others. The saints at Corinth constituted his endorsement. They were his credentials. "Ye are our epistle written

82

in our hearts, known and read of all men"
(2 Corinthians 3:2; KJV). The Corinthian
saints were an epistle of Christ and the
only letter of commendation required by
Paul. "Truly the signs of an apostle were
wrought among you in all patience, in
signs, and wonders, and mighty deeds"
(12:12). What was engraved upon their
hearts by his apostolic labor could be read
by all men who would certainly know that
an apostle of Christ had planted the congregation.

"Forasmuch as ye are manifestly declared to be the epistle of Christ ministered
by us, written not with ink, but with the
Spirit of the living God; not in tables of
stone, but in fleshy tables of the heart"
(3:3; KJV). Here we have the contrast between the "old covenant" and the "new."
The saints are the living letters of the living God. They are the epistles of Christ.
Jesus is the author, the apostles His tran-
scribers. They ministered the epistle because God had made them "able ministers
of the new testament" (v. 6).

The new covenant was not written with
ink. It is not a written code. It does not consist of the Gospels, the book of Acts, the
epistles, and Revelation. Every one of
these books was written with ink. John's
epistles were written with paper and ink (2
John 12) and with pen and ink (3 John 13).
These were written to a covenant people,

but they are not part of the covenant. That covenant was engraved by the Spirit of God, "not in tables of stone, but in fleshy tables of the heart."

This is exactly what God promised through Jeremiah. "I will put my laws into their mind, and write them in their hearts: and I will be to them a God, and they shall be to me a people" (Hebrews 8:10; KJV). The new covenant is not an external code. It cannot be read on tablets of stone or in a book written with pen and ink. In spite of the plain statements of God's Word that we are not under law, and that the new covenant was not written with ink, it is difficult for many persons to see how God's *laws* can be put into the mind or written in the heart, if we are not under law.

The answer lies in the fact that the word "law" has a wide range of meanings. When we read that we are not under law, the apostle is not telling us that we are no longer under the sovereignty of God, but that we are no longer under a written code or legalistic system. We can no longer strive for justification, or seek to arrive at guiltlessness, by observance of such a code laid down or imposed from without. Law, in its primal meaning, is a principle of action. It is the basis, or foundation, the motivating dynamic that governs our whole course of conduct.

God does not write numbered statutes

and commandments upon our hearts as the Romans engraved laws upon the twelve bronze tablets in the Forum, or as His finger carved the Ten Commandments upon two tablets of stone at Sinai. Instead, He infuses our hearts with a divine principle of action, and this spontaneously and automatically responds in harmony with His will. Incorporated within that principle, which involves the divine nature or essence, is the fulfillment of all the commands of God, not as a way of life, but as "the life of the Way."

It is for this reason Paul writes, in contrasting the old covenant with the new, that God made the apostles the qualified ambassadors or administrative agents of the "new testament" or covenant. That covenant was not based upon a written code, but upon the Spirit, because a written code can only terminate in death. Instead, the Spirit gives life. Law says, "Do these things and you shall live." The Spirit says, "You live, so do these things." The law starts with man as he is, inducing him to seek to achieve life by his effort. "For Moses describeth the righteousness which is of the law, That the man which doeth those things shall live by them" (Romans 10:5; KJV).

In plain language this means that under a regime of law, life is dependent upon human performance. Law must be kept

85

meticulously or it is not kept at all. The slightest infraction results in death. The "fly in the ointment" is the fact that man in the flesh cannot keep law perfectly. It is an impossibility, not because of the weakness of the law, but because of the weakness of the flesh. A system based upon law-keeping can never produce righteousness or justification. "Therefore by the deeds of the law there shall no flesh be justified in his sight: for by the law is the knowledge of sin" (Romans 3:20). *No flesh!* Law can make men aware of their weakness and sin. It can produce a sense of failure and guilt upon the part of those who seek to submit to it. Never can it produce guiltlessness in any person who is in the flesh!

Life is not a product of law. No written code, regardless of its origin, can ever produce life. If life could result from law-keeping, it was a heinous act for God to send Christ to die for our sins. He should have sent the law, or given the written code that could produce life. Paul writes, "If there had been a law given which could have given life, verily righteousness should have been by the law" (Galatians 3:21). He also writes, "If righteousness come by the law, then Christ is dead in vain" (2:21).

The Spirit does not start with man as he is, but when that man trusts in the righteousness of God, which is through faith in Christ Jesus, the Spirit makes of him a new creation. He is dead, and his life is "hid with Christ in God" (Colossians 3:3; KJV). Christ becomes his life, for he has no life of his own. His life is not dependent upon obedience to laws, but because he has been transformed he keeps the commands of Christ who is his life. His service is not an attempt to keep the law, but to conform to the Spirit. He is not in the flesh but in the Spirit, because the Spirit of Christ abides in him.

Those who are in Christ are dead to the principles of legalistic righteousness. The custodian who held them is dead. His nerveless grasp has been broken from their necks. Now they are delivered and freed from a written code. That basis of justification is deceased, declared invalid by God's marvelous grace. The purpose is that all of us should serve in newness of spirit and not in the oldness of a written code. This, I think, is what Paul is saying in Romans 7:6: "Now we are delivered from the law, that being dead wherein we were held; that we should serve in newness of spirit, and not in the oldness of the letter" (KJV). There is no intimation that service to God is relaxed because the principle of legalistic rectitude is dead. We serve, but it is in newness of spirit. Just because we have matured and the custodian is dead, these facts do not lessen our responsibility. Our very maturity increases that responsibility.

At this point we must inquire as to the principle that is put in our mind and written in our heart, which constitutes the new covenant rule of action. Paul's letters to the Romans and the Galatians are two great dissertations on the difference between law and faith as grounds of justification. It is in these letters the apostle plainly enunciates the one great quality that embraces and fulfills all law.

First let us look at the Roman letter. In it we are told, "Owe no man any thing, but to love one another: for he that loveth another hath fulfilled the law. For this, Thou shalt not commit adultery, Thou shalt not kill, Thou shalt not steal, Thou shalt not bear false witness, Thou shalt not covet; and if there be any other commandment, it is briefly comprehended in this saying, namely, Thou shalt love thy neighbour as thyself. Love worketh no ill to his neighbour: therefore love is the fulfilling of the law" (Romans 13:8-10; KJV).

Obviously, the whole purpose of any law given by God is to establish a right relationship with himself and with men. But law cannot accomplish this because law can only make one conscious of failure and guilt. It cannot make him guiltless. Law is external. Love is internal. When one is justified by faith, which is the only way he can be justified, he attains peace with God through the Lord Jesus Christ. Through

Jesus he gains access to grace, in which state he can rejoice in hope of the glory of God. This hope never disappoints the one who is at one with God, "because the love of God is shed abroad in our hearts by the Holy Ghost which is given unto us" (Romans 5:5).

The first covenant was one of law, the second is one of love. The only debt I can owe another, which it is impossible to settle in full, is that of love. I must never borrow from another what I cannot repay. I do not love God's children because I am in debt to them, but because I am in debt to Him. "Let us love one another: for love is of God" (1 John 4:7); "Beloved, if God so loved us, we ought also to love one another" (v. 11). One should emphasize the word "so" in this statement.

Love fulfills the law. The apostle specifically mentions five Commandments, forbidding adultery, murder, stealing, false testimony, and covetousness. We generally think of these as moral regulations, but lest the legalistic mind try to find an exception, he writes, "And if there be any other commandment." No law can be given to cover every facet of human behavior or every contingency. Faith in Jesus lifts us out of the area of written codes and shows us "the more excellent way."

Love fulfills the law *because it works no ill to another*. The love that is here contemplated is the unceasing, undying, uninhibited concern for another's good, manifesting itself in positive action to promote that good. That active and beneficent good will stops at nothing to achieve the good of the beloved object. It is the application of the new God-nature to all human circumstances, problems of association and relationship. Such a broad scope as this can never be captured or confined by a written code, any more than such a code can contain the very essence of God.

For fifteen hundred years God sought to hold His people together by law, until faith could come. Law is a police force, drawing a circle and building a fence beyond which the inmates must not go, under penalty of death or banishment. When Jesus came, law was abandoned as basis of unity, and love was installed in its place. Love is a magnetic force, holding men together by drawing them to a common center. That center is the person of Jesus, who announced, "And I, if I be lifted up from the earth, will draw all men unto me."

Jesus did not confine us with another law. He did not build another fence. He did not provide another yoke of bondage. Instead, He set us free, He freed us, not only from the law given by Moses, but the law principle that is helpless because of the flesh. We are told, "Stand fast therefore in the liberty wherewith Christ hath made us free, and be not entangled again with the yoke of bondage" (Galatians 5:1; KJV). Any man who postulates his hope of glory upon conformity to a written code is signing his own death warrant. He is building his own scaffold and knotting his own hangman's noose. It makes no difference whether he conceives of the written code as originating with God or man.

"For, brethren, ye have been called unto liberty; only use not liberty for an occasion to the flesh, but by love serve one another. For all the law is fulfilled in one word, even in this; Thou shalt love thy neighbour as thyself" (5:13, 14; KJV). Here the apostle says the same thing to the emotional Gauls that he wrote to the Romans. In doing so, he defines the true use of liberty. Those who are freed from definitive written codes full of "thou shalt nots" are sometimes inclined to take advantage of their liberty. Because there is no wall to debar their progress, they may strain and break the cord of love that holds them to the center—the cross.

We have been called to liberty, but it is not our achievement. We did not escape from prison, we were liberated. We did not disentangle ourselves from the yoke; it was lifted from us. We have been called, so we have a vocation of liberty. We dare not use our God-given liberty to serve the flesh. The custodian died only after delivering us to Jesus. We are not free to do as we please; we are now free to do what will please Him. Liberty and service occur in the same context. "Ye have been called unto liberty ... by love serve one another" (v. 13).

The new covenant has been inscribed on the walls of the heart. It has not been written with ink but with the Spirit. It does not consist of a compilation of legal propositions, but of one word: love! Correctly understood, that word involves all that law was intended to accomplish but could not. It lifts man out of the very domain of law. It places him in a realm where he can bear the fruits of the Spirit. "Against such there is no law" (v. 23). *No law!*

Love fulfills the law *because it removes stumbling blocks.* Love takes away every occasion for stumbling; that is, it creates no hazard, obstacle, or obstruction to cause anyone to trip or fall. Love is light, hatred is darkness. "He that loveth his brother abideth in the light, and there is none occasion of stumbling in him" (1 John 2:10).

Love fulfills the law *because it gives assurance of life.* Love assures us that we have crossed the frontier separating death from life. No written code could ever do this. Under a written code one can never be sure he has gone far enough or done enough to be counted worthy of life. He can never be certain there is not something he should have known and did not know, or something he should have done and did not do. Under the law of love, "We know that we have passed from death unto life, because we love the brethren" (1 John 3:14). Love for the brethren is not the ferry that transports us from death to life. That ferry is faith. But the ability to "love the brethren" is on the opposite side of the border from death. When we have achieved that goal we know we are across the line, because love is the proof of the indwelling Spirit. "And hereby we know that we are of the truth, and shall assure our hearts before him" (v. 19).

Love is the fulfilling of the law *because God dwells within us.* "If we love one another, God dwelleth in us, and his love is perfected in us" (4:12; KJV). When God gave the old covenant it was deposited in a sacred ark. It was kept in an earthly sanctuary constructed by the hands of men. Today we are the only sanctuary God has on earth. The covenant cannot be borne upon the shoulders of a special caste. It is enshrined in the hearts of believers. We are the temple of God. Our bodies are His tabernacle. We cannot carry the covenant in our hands. It is not a book we can lay on the library table or place on the shelf. The new covenant is a pact of love. It exhibits itself in love for one another. It is the love of God perfected, fulfilled, and matured.

Under the new covenant God dwells in us

93

and we dwell in Him, because He has given us His Spirit (v. 13). The Spirit is life-giving because He is love-giving. We live because we love, and we love because we live. There is no life apart from love. God is love, and His love is manifested toward us because He "sent His only begotten Son into the world, that we might live through him" (v. 9). As John adds, "Herein is love," so we may add, "Herein is life."

The first covenant was announced at a physical mount; the new covenant at a spiritual peak in man's history. When the first was announced, those who heard it were cautioned not to draw near or to cross a boundary. When the second was given, they were invited to "Draw near with a true heart in full assurance" (Hebrews 10:22). The first was engraved upon stone, and was as inflexible as the material upon which it was carved. The second was written upon the hearts of believers, and was as warm as the faith that led them to receive Jesus. The first bound the recipients to God upon the threat that the iniquities of the fathers would be visited upon the children to the third and fourth generations. The second drew the respondents by the promise that their sins would be remembered no more forever. Truly it is a "better covenant, based upon better promises"!

# Chapter 9

# THE FREEDOM OF MATURITY

It is extremely difficult for many conse-crated believers in Christ to accept the im-plications of the material in the preceding chapter. There are several reasons why this is so. For one thing, it cuts across the traditional pattern of teaching. We have always been told that "the new testament" consists of twenty-seven books. It seems almost heretical for one to say this is not true. To refute it seems to deny God's Word, even though God nowhere said or implied that such was the case.

It cannot be denied that thousands of people in the world, both Jews and Greeks, were in covenant relationship with God be-fore one word of the New Covenant Scrip-tures was ever written. Many who died for the faith had never seen an apostolic letter. Many had no idea there would ever be a compilation of such letters. They simply be-lieved that Jesus was the Messiah and God's Son, and pledged allegiance to Him. They renounced any thought of their own righteousness as having been attained by works of the law, and simply put their trust in the righteousness of God through faith in Christ Jesus.

The divine agreement, the covenant that established their relationship with the Father of all mercy, was inscribed by the Holy Spirit upon the walls of the inner chambers of their being. It was written in terms of love, a dynamic so powerful that it not only transformed their lives but completely altered the world in which they lived. The New Covenant Scriptures, now entitled the New Testament, grew out of their covenantal relationship, not vice versa.

As time went on, the Holy Spirit motivated certain ones to make a record of the divine breakthrough on the human plane. A former tax-collector told the story primarily for the Jews. A young man who grew up in Jersualem, a close friend of Simon Peter, wrote it for the Romans and the Latin world. A Greek physician interviewed eyewitnesses and then compiled and collated the information he had received for presentation to a Greek state official. To this he later added and certified an account of the struggle of the message of hope to free itself, first from the bonds of Jewish legalism, and second from the toils of Greek philosophy. The account ends with the proclamation free and the proclaimer in prison. Much later, a former fisherman, who survived all of the other apostles, wrote a supplementary account to offset the effects of one of the most subtle foes that ever sought to infiltrate the faith.

As communities of believers were beset with problems growing out of the humanity of the covenant people, the apostles wrote letters to them, furnishing guidelines for rethinking their conduct. Sometimes these grew out of reports received from persons who were familiar with the saints in a given locality. Other times they were replies to letters that had asked for information. In still other circumstances the apostles wrote simply because the situation warranted it. One of these was a letter commending a runaway slave to his master, to whose home he was returning. Another was addressed to a people who were being seduced from the liberty they enjoyed in Jesus.

Those who received the letters did not regard them as legal documents. The writers who penned them had no consciousness of creating a code of laws. They merely wrote letters of deep affection to people whom they loved, without any thought of writing a Bible. Paul, who wrote most of the letters, disclaimed any thought of domination over the faith of the recipients. He said, "Not for that we have dominion over your faith, but are helpers of your joy: for by faith ye stand" (2 Corinthians 1:24; KJV).

During the life span of the apostles, the letters were scattered among isolated communities, although they were occasionally shared with other believers in the same general region (Colossians 4:16). It was not until long after the death of John, and after a good deal of debate about the validity of some of the letters, that the canon was completed and the New Covenant Scriptures were collected as we now have them.

It is true that our relationship to God is a covenantal relationship. There is a great deal of difference, however, between the covenant or agreement and the letters written to the covenant people. The covenant is entered by faith in Jesus as the fulfillment of the promises of God. It results from a response to the good news that Christ "hath abolished death, and hath brought life and immortality to light through the gospel" (2 Timothy 1:10). The gospel was fully proclaimed on Pentecost. Not another word was ever added to it. Those who responded to it, by reformation of life and baptism, entered into the covenant with God, even though they never saw an apostolic letter and certainly never saw a copy of the New Covenant Scriptures.

The gospel is not a legalistic arrangement by which we earn God's favor. It is the good news of God's marvelous grace growing out of the love which God is. The

98

New Covenant Scriptures are not a legalistic code, for we are not under law but under grace. The Scriptures are a collection of "love letters," written in familiar terms. They do not represent the will of God imposed, but the mind of God exposed. They act as guidelines, showing how Christ would react under conditions faced by saints on earth. They are instructional material intended to inform subjects how to prepare for the coming of their King.

Another reason for the reluctance of many people to accept what was said about the covenants is that they would rather be under law than under grace. It is for this reason they make grace into law and convert the love letters of the apostles into a written code. They are frightened by the freedom that makes them personally responsible for their decisions. They prefer to have things "spelled out" and have a lawbook. Then they can go and "look it up" to see how far they can go and still remain within the limits. It is easier to qualify as a good lawyer than as a great lover. It is easier to lay down the law than to live up to love.

This is indicative of emotional and spiritual immaturity. An adolescent outwardly demands freedom but inwardly craves restraint. He wants his parents to lay down laws, even though he professes outward rebellion against their regulations. The reason for this inner turmoil is his association of love with law. Enforcement of law, even though it galls him to comply, indicates to his still immature mind that his parents are shielding and protecting him from the big world he is still afraid to face alone. He would rather be behind walls with a sense of security than to be forced to face life openly and on his own.

In the Roman world in which the apostles lived, a son was turned over to others who were charged with his rearing. Even though the boy was destined to become heir to his father's estate and title of nobility, he was under such a tight reign and subjected to such strict discipline that he was little better off than a slave. Every action was ordered by others. His life was regimented each hour of the day. He made no independent decisions. All of this continued until he reached the age of puberty, when his father publicly presented him as a citizen to the populace.

The whole course of a youth's life was changed from that moment onward. No longer was he under the hand of disciplinarians who could flog him into compliance with their will. Publicly recognized as a son by the father, he could now move among men as a man. This did not mean he was a law unto himself. He was bound by ties of respect to his family. His actions brought honor or dishonor to the family name. His concern had to be for others. He had to measure his behavior in the light of his influence.

Paul uses this familiar way of life to illustrate God's plan for His people through the ages. After describing the law as a custodian charged with delivering us to Christ, and pointing out that once this was accomplished we were no longer under a custodian, he introduces the example drawn from social life: "Now I say, That the heir, as long as he is a child, differeth nothing from a servant, though he be lord of all; but is under tutors and governors until the time appointed of the father" (Galatians 4:1, 2; KJV).

Notice now his application to the people of God: "Even so we, when we were children, were in bondage under the elements of the world" (v. 3). In their childhood age, God's chosen people were treated as children. At Mount Sinai they were placed under the tutelage of a custodian. That custodian was the written code. This stern disciplinarian actually reduced the children to a status comparable to that of household slaves. The written code is here referred to as "the elements of this world." The term refers to the fundamental or primary principles upon which any system is founded. In the literary world it was applied to the alphabet, which was basic to all writing. In the natural world it was applied to atoms out of which all matter was composed. In the social world it was applied to fundamentals of moral and ethical behavior.

"But when the fulness of the time was come, God sent forth his Son, made of a woman, made under the law, to redeem them that were under the law, that we might receive the adoption of sons" (vv. 4, 5). Under Roman law the father decided the time when he would deliver the son from his custodians, and publicly acknowledge him as a son of the family and a citizen of the commonwealth. In the spiritual realm, it was God who ordained the time when faith should come.

When the time arrived for the world's attainment of sonship, God sent His Son. It was important that our deliverance be wrought by the Son, because in Him we could see what was entailed in divine sonship. The Son of God became the Son of man so that the sons of men could become the sons of God. Note that God did not send a new or better legal code to deliver us. Instead, He sent His Son. In Christ we do not sustain a legal relationship to the Father, but a personal one. God sent a person to inaugurate that relationship.

In His entrance into our world to share our lot, Jesus was made of a woman. He was not the seed of man. He was not begotten by Joseph, although He was conceived

102

by Mary. He was made under the law, and He fulfilled it. He was the only person who ever did so. He was tempted in all points as we are, but He was without sin. Because He had no sin for which to suffer, He could suffer for our sins. God laid upon Him the iniquity of us all. He delivered us from the curse of the law by having been made a curse for us.

It is through Christ's sacrifice that we receive the adoption of sons. "And because ye are sons, God hath sent forth the Spirit of His Son into your hearts, crying, Abba, Father. Wherefore thou art no more a servant, but a son; and if a son, then an heir of God through Christ" (vv. 6, 7). God did not hand us another law, a written code to govern us as sons. Such a code belonged to the days of childish immaturity. He sent forth the Spirit of His Son, that is, the Spirit of sonship. The Holy Spirit's indwelling presence marks us out as belonging to the divine family.

The Spirit within brings out the consciousness of a father-son relationship. It is not based upon legalistic compliance but upon acceptance through mutuality of love. "We love him, because he first loved us," wrote John (1 John 4:19). In the joy of acceptance, expressed by the word "adoption," the inner being cries out "Abba, Father." The first term expresses the initial exclamation of the little child for the

103

parent, conveying affection and dependence. The last is the mature recognition of warm relationship.

God has delivered us from the status of slaves. He no longer treats us as minors. The coming of Jesus was the signal for the coming of age of the people of God. The fullness of the time was the time of their fullness. Unfortunately, many people are not able to accept the sense of responsibility involved in the freedom of sonship. In their spiritual adolescence they seek to convert the very love letters addressed to them into a legalistic arrangement, which would thrust them back into slavery.

Only a little thought is required to demonstrate that the new covenant cannot be postulated upon such a written code. When a community is founded upon law, the law must be enunciated first. Those who are to constitute the community must consent to it and pledge their allegiance to it. If the procedure were the reverse of this, the community could have imposed upon it regulations that the members would abhor, and to which they could not subscribe in good conscience. As was stated, we do not erect a structure and then construct a foundation; we first lay the foundation.

The nation of Israel is a good example. It was God's design to create for himself a nation that would preserve the concept of monotheism until the Messiah should come. He would be identified as the Son of the one God who made Heaven and earth. Accordingly, God called His people out of slavery in Egypt and led them across the Red Sea. Instead of taking them by the ancient caravan route, which gave direct access to the land of Canaan but led through hostile Philistine territory, He conducted them southward to Mount Sinai, or Horeb. He called Moses to come up into the mountain in the presence of all the people and gave him instructions to relay to the multitude. The people were to wash their clothes so they could appear clean in the presence of the Lord. They were to abstain from sexual relationship with their wives. They were not to touch the mountain, under the penalty of death. A boundary line was drawn around the base of the mountain so no man or beast could make physical contact with it. Then, "Moses brought forth the people out of the camp to meet with God" (Exodus 19:17; KJV).

When the assembly heard the voice of God thundering from the peak, they were frightened. They requested that Moses be allowed to go and receive the message of God and relay it to them. "And Moses came and told the people all the words of the Lord, and all the judgments: and all the people answered with one voice, and said, All the words which the Lord hath said will we do" (Exodus 24:3).

Moses wrote all the words God had spoken, and arose very early in the morning to construct an altar in the shadow of the hill. Young men were dispatched to offer a sacrifice upon the altar. Moses caught half of the blood in a basin and sprinkled the remainder upon the altar to sanctify it. He then took the book of the covenant and read it in the hearing of the people. They responded to the reading by saying, "All that the Lord hath said will we do, and be obedient" (v. 7). Moses thereupon took the blood in the basin and sprinkled it upon the people and the book, saying, "Behold the blood of the covenant, which the Lord hath made with you concerning all these words" (v. 8).

The sprinkling of the book consecrated it to the people, while the sprinkling of the people consecrated them to the book. The covenant founded upon law was inaugurated, and from thenceforth the nation was bound to keep all the words of that law or die. To violate a covenant with God is a tragic renunciation of a promise. To break a covenant with Him is to become a traitor to the Eternal God.

In the case of the "new covenant," which God specifically declared was not to be like the one made with the fathers when they were led forth from Egypt, there was no written code announced and read. Ours is a personal relationship with Jesus, through

106

whom grace and truth came. Instead of writing a book and sprinkling it with blood, Peter publicly announced the facts concerning the life, death, burial, and resurrection of Jesus. He ended by saying, "This same Jesus God raised up and made Him both Lord and Christ." The application of the blood of the new covenant was figuratively to the hearts of the believers.

The New Covenant Scriptures could not have constituted a legal code upon which the church was erected, simply because they were not yet written. They were written many years later. It is true that those who were baptized "continued stedfastly in the teaching of the apostles," also in the sharing of the common life in Christ, in the breaking of bread, and in prayers, but this was in no sense a ritualistic performance based upon legal specifications. It was the natural expression of hearts filled with the Holy Spirit after being cleansed and purged by divine forgiveness.

A written code was the foundation of the nation composed of those called out from slavery in Egypt. The foundation of the kingdom composed of those called out of bondage to sin was a simple fact, the greatest in all history. That fact is that Jesus is the Messiah, the Son of the living God. When Simon Peter openly testified to it, Jesus pronounced a blessing upon him and declared that his statement was a

Heaven-revealed truth. He said, "Upon this rock I will build my church." On that fact He would plant the called-out ones. The church is composed of those who are not under law, but under grace. Their hope is not derived from righteousness based upon law, but from righteousness of faith in Christ.

At one time in my life I thought the New Covenant Scriptures, consisting of the apostolic letters of love and sharing, constituted a blueprint for the church, exactly as the legal code given at Sinai did for the nation of Israel. I did not stop to realize that a blueprint must be in the hands of the construction superintendent and the carpenters before the building is started. I freely quoted what God said to Moses when he was about to make the tabernacle, and applied it to ourselves. The instruction to Moses was "See ... that thou make all things according to the pattern shewed to thee in the mount" (Hebrews 8:5; KJV).

In spite of what may be said about "pattern theology" and a "divine blueprint," the New Covenant Scriptures do not constitute either a pattern or blueprint by which the church was constructed. If they do, the church was not built by the blueprint, because it was in existence a good many years before a single epistle was written. Each letter was addressed to only one community of believers. Not one area had all of the Scriptures available to it for many decades. There were congregations that lived and perished who never saw one segment of "the blueprint," and did not know that such existed.

The writer of Hebrews contrasts the old covenant and the new. Unfortunately, many readers think he is comparing them and pointing out similarities. Reference is made to the time when Moses was instructed to build the tabernacle after having been shown a pattern of the tent and all of its furnishings. Many readers assume that when God said, "See that you make all things according to the pattern," He was, by implication, telling us also to build the church according to a blueprint supplied to and by the apostles. This analogy breaks down for several reasons, including the following:

1. Moses was given a preview of the tabernacle because it was to be built by men who had never seen such a structure. It is specifically stated, however, that the true tabernacle was one "which the Lord pitched, and not man" (8:2). Since it was not pitched by man, it was unnecessary to provide a blueprint for man.

2. Since the priests offered gifts according to the law and served "unto the example and shadow of heavenly things," it is sometimes argued that we are under a

written blueprint to provide the antitype. In that eventuality our blueprint would have been the pattern shown to Moses, not the New Covenant Scriptures at all. Our task would be to "spiritualize" the pattern shown to Moses and to erect the true tabernacle accordingly. In that case the true tabernacle would be pitched by man, and not the Lord, in contravention of the plain Scriptural statement.

3. The very next sentence after the quotation relating to the "pattern shown to Moses" (v. 5), begins with the words, "But now." When these words occur in Scripture, they indicate a change in God's dealings with mankind. It is true that under the first covenant Moses was shown a replica of the tabernacle and instructed to make everything according to it. The writer of Hebrews continues, "But now hath he [Christ] obtained a more excellent ministry, by how much also he is the mediator of a better covenant, which was established upon better promises" (v. 6).

Under the new covenant God did not provide a pattern or blueprint of a structure. Instead, He gave His Son, and it is the Son who is our pattern, or example. Speaking about the persecution and hardship that are to be endured by one who is identified with Jesus, Peter writes, "For even hereunto were ye called: because Christ also suffered for us, leaving us an example, that ye should follow his steps" (1 Peter 2:21; KJV).

The temple of God today is composed of living stones, of individuals who are cleansed and purified by the blood of Christ. The only sanctuary is a consecrated human heart, and for this the blueprint is the life of Jesus. The first covenant began with a book; the new covenant began with a baby. The first created holy days and holy places, the second created holy persons. The first covenant, like the first Adam, was of the earth, earthy; the second covenant, like the second Adam, was the Lord from Heaven.

Our hope lies in conformity to the Christ, not in conformity to a code. We do not walk in statutes but in the Spirit. We are free from the demands of the flesh, which made law necessary. The flesh has no claim upon us, since Jesus died in the flesh. Those who continue to walk after the flesh shall die. We are not in the flesh but in the Spirit, if it is true that the Spirit of Christ dwells in us. When the dominion of the flesh was destroyed and we were liberated, we were freed from the bondage in which we were once held. To form a new written code from the letters that the apostles wrote to congregations and individuals, would be to forge anew the fetters that would bring us once again into captivity to law.

Chapter 10

# ANSWERING OBJECTIONS

It would be both unfair and unwise to pretend that there are no objections to the position advocated in this volume. The fact is that serious questions are raised, and many of these come from sincere students of the divine revelation. They love truth and are eager seekers after it. They do not want to be misled or diverted into a false path. Their questions deserve careful consideration and demand honest answers.

First, let us give attention to those passages of the apostolic letters which seem to indicate we are still under law. Paul clearly states, "By works of the law no flesh shall be justified in his [God's] sight" (Romans 3:20). He also declares that we are "not under the law, but under grace" (6:14). If the very letters Paul wrote constitute a written code, and compose part of the framework of a legalistic system, it is obvious that we are still under law. The apostle then contradicts himself.

It will help us to keep in mind that the word "law" covers a wide spectrum of thought. The term itself is from an Old English form that refers to something laid or fixed, without reference to the source of the action. Our modern word "lay" is directly related to it, and we still use the expression, "lay down the law," when we speak of someone disclosing his wishes in an authoritative fashion.

In the New Covenant Scriptures the Greek word is *nomos,* and this refers to any rule of action, including that which motivates or impels one to engage in certain actions. Perhaps the term "controlling principle" sums up the wide scope of meanings. In this sense all are under law as the natural consequence of being rational, or having the power to reason. Paul affirms, "When Gentiles who have not the law do by nature what the law requires, they are a law to themselves, even though they do not have the law. They show that what the law requires is written on their hearts, while their conscience also bears witness and their conflicting thoughts accuse or perhaps excuse them on that day when, according to my gospel, God judges the secrets of men by Christ Jesus" (Romans 2:14-16; RSV).

In this same connection he asserts, "So, if a man who is uncircumcised keeps the precepts of the law, will not his uncircumcision be regarded as circumcision? Then those who are physically uncircumcised but keep the law will condemn you who have the written code and circumcision but break the law" (vv. 26, 27; RSV). A clear distinction is thus made between the written code and the principles of conduct observed as a natural result of our status as human beings, which provides us with both the power to think and the restraint of conscience. Every sane person acts through motivation or impulse, and the principles governing his action can be properly called law. It is obvious that those who have crucified the old man of sin and who are made partakers of the divine nature will act as directed and motivated by that nature, being a part of "the new humanity."

The question that concerns us is whether or not under the benign dominion of grace we are still under a legalistic system. Do the New Covenant Scriptures constitute a written code in the sense that the writings of Moses constituted such a code? Are we justified by conformity to a written code? Is grace simply the substitution of a new written code of laws for another that was declared invalid? This is precisely what a great many people think, and it is the reason why every use of the word "law" is interpreted by them to indicate that we are still under a legalistic system.

A good case in point is found in Romans 3:27, where Paul speaks of "the law of faith." Simple attention to the context should demonstrate that the apostle is not referring to a written code. Certainly the collection of New Covenant Scriptures cannot possibly constitute "the law of faith" of which he speaks.

Paul affirms that the righteousness of God to which the law and the prophets testified is now seen to be achieved without the law, and this is through faith in Jesus Christ (vv. 21-23). Upon this basis it is available to all who believe in Him, and there is no difference or distinction, since all have sinned and fallen short of the glory of God.

Paul further makes it clear that justification is by grace, which is a gift, freely given through the wonderful redemption in Christ Jesus. No longer does man identify with law in a vain hope of attaining righteousness, but with Christ Jesus who is our righteousness.

Paul anticipates the question, "Where is boasting then?" (v. 27). The answer is that it is excluded. It is obvious that if one attained to righteousness by his own efforts, through proper understanding and implementation of all the demands of law, he would have grounds to boast of his accomplishment. On the other hand, if righteousness is a gift based wholly upon what another has done for him, and which he could not do for himself, he has no reason for pride or boasting. The apostle writes, "Where is boasting then? It is excluded. By what law? of works? Nay: but by the law of faith" (v. 27; KJV).

It is regrettable that the *King James Version* has the rendering "law," since the apostle is dealing with the principle of justification. There are but two conceivable bases upon which justification can be predicated. One is the perfect keeping of law, and the other is absolute trust in a perfect Redeemer. The first is impossible for men in the flesh, the second negates human pride and boasting. The *Revised Standard Version* is correct in rendering the passage, "Then what becomes of our boasting? It is excluded. On what principle? On the principle of works? No, but on the principle of faith." The next verse states the conclusion, "For we hold that a man is justified by faith apart from works of law."

Certainly the "law of faith," as the term is employed in the *King James Version*, has no relation to a written code. The Romans who received the letter never saw a copy of the New Covenant Scriptures. To postulate to them that they were to be justified by conformity to such a compilation of letters would have confused them as much as it does those in our generation who have inserted their own interpretation of Paul's words. The principle of faith in the righteousness of Jesus Christ is one thing; the letters addressed to those who are in Him constitute a wholly different thing.

Romans 8 also causes concern for those who think of a written code every time they see the word "law." The apostle Paul writes, "There is therefore now no condemnation to them which are in Christ Jesus, who walk not after the flesh, but after the Spirit. For the law of the Spirit of life in Christ Jesus hath made me free from the law of sin and death" (vv. 1, 2).

Those who equate "the law of sin and death" with the legalistic code given at Sinai tend to think of "the law of the Spirit of life" as being the New Covenant Scriptures. This is another example of reading into the Scriptures an opinion reflecting a postapostolic conclusion. The apostle stated in the previous chapter that we were freed from the demands of the law, having died to that which held us captive. Now we serve God, not under the old written code, but in the new life of the Spirit. One who is in Christ Jesus is freed from condemnation. There is no condemnation in Christ. He atoned for our sins on the cross, redeemed us from iniquity, and removed our guilt.

It is true that the Spirit inspired and empowered those who wrote the Scriptures, but it is not the Scriptures to which the apostle here alludes. He is saying that the principle of "the Spirit of life in Christ Jesus" has set us free and delivered us from the dominion of sin and death. Life in

117

Christ is the natural order for the redeemed ones. The law of the Spirit is not a book but life in Christ Jesus. Those to whom Paul wrote were walking according to that law of the Spirit long before they received the letter he penned.

Properly understood, this explains the term "law of God" in the seventh verse, where Paul said, "The carnal mind is enmity against God: for it is not subject to the law of God, neither indeed can be." The carnal mind is the mind of the flesh, the rational part of man under the dominating principle of the corrupt nature. Such a mind is not merely apathetic to the will of God, but antagonistic and hostile. The alienation that results from the lower nature breeds enmity against God.

In 1 Corinthians 9:21 the apostle declares he is "not without law to God, but under the law of Christ" (KJV). Those persons who regard the New Covenant Scriptures as a written code project that idea into the expression, "under the law to Christ." This is the result of forgetting or ignoring the context of the passage and Paul's purpose of writing it.

In the preceding verses the apostle had outlined his reasons for not accepting financial support from the Corinthians, a right he abdicated rather than suffer under the accusation that he was proclaiming the gospel for personal gain. His complete adherence to the will of Christ made him free from any claim men might exercise over him. In spite of the fact that he was free from all men, he made himself a slave to all, adapting and accommodating himself to others, so that he might influence them to come to Christ.

"To them that are under the law, as under the law, that I might gain them that are under the law" (v. 20). This refers to the law given by Moses. When Paul labored among those who were scrupulous in keeping the law, he did not offend them by deliberately flaunting its provisions. He moved within its regulations. Once, while in Jerusalem, he acted upon the counsel of James to prove that he personally lived in observance of the law (Acts 21:24). When among Jews, Paul lived as a Jewish national; when among those under the law, he conducted himself as one subservient to the demands of the law.

"To them that are without law, as without law, (being not without law to God, but under the law to Christ,) that I might gain them that are without law" (v. 21). The term *anomos*, which would be properly rendered "lawless," does not apply to the conduct or character of the people. It refers to the fact that no law had been given them or enacted for them. There is a difference in being without law and being an outlaw. It is a tribute to the versatility and flexibility of Paul that he could fit into the daily life of non-Jews.

The apostle did not want the Corinthians to think that he was antinomian, that is, opposed to rules of life and conduct. He was not a scofflaw. Even while living among those who had not received oracles from God, he recognized the sovereignty of God over every facet of life. He acknowledged also the fact that all authority had been given to Christ. In fact, Christ was Paul's law, the life of Jesus being his example and pattern. None of this argues that the new covenant is another legal code or that the New Covenant Scriptures constitute a legal document rather than a disclosure of the nature of grace.

Perhaps one of the most interesting studies in this regard is the letter of James, addressed directly "To the twelve tribes in the Dispersion" (James 1:1; RSV). That these were Jews who believed in Jesus as the Messiah is quite clear from James 2:1, 2. The word "assembly" is from *sunagoge* rather than from *ekklesia*. James speaks to them of the "perfect law" (1:25), the "royal law" (2:8), and the "law of liberty" (1:25). That all of these expressions refer to the same thing is at once apparent to the careful reader.

James begins in 1:22 with the solemn admonition that men must be doers of what is enjoined by the Word of God, and not mere hearers. Hearers of the Word only serve to deceive themselves. They listen but do not learn. In common parlance they allow what they hear to "go into one ear and out of the other." The writer declares that such a person is like a man who looks into a mirror and immediately forgets what he was like. Such a man would not remove marks or blemishes from his countenance, because he has forgotten about them.

This is followed by a contrast, quoted from the *Revised Standard Version*, because this reading seems to best grasp the meaning of the original: "But he who looks into the perfect law, the law of liberty, and perseveres, being no hearer that forgets but a doer that acts, he shall be blessed in his doing" (v. 25). What is the "perfect law"? It could not be the completed New Covenant Scriptures, of which the letter by James is a part, because there was no such compilation at the time. It is probable that the addressees of "the Dispersion" never saw another apostolic letter. Some of them, scattered as exiles throughout Asia Minor, may have read the letter designated "the First Epistle of Peter."

The "perfect law" is not a designation for the completed canon of the New Covenant Scriptures. Those who received the letter from James would have been in their graves many years before there was such a collection of apostolic documents. The word

121

"perfect" is applied to "the law of liberty" because of its origin. It is from God and was personified in Christ. It was personal rather than preceptual, providing a Savior rather than statutes. The perfect law was embodied in a Man rather than inscribed in a manual. It was the life of Christ rather than a list of codes. Christ Jesus has left us an example that we should follow in His steps (1 Peter 2:21). The perfect law is from the mind of a perfect God, and was lived out before us in a sinless life.

The "law of liberty" is also perfect because of its nature. It is the law of love, and this love is the very essence of God. *God is love*. Every commandment is summed up in love, so that the one who truly loves fulfills every demand for which law was intended. Love validates every gift and sanctifies every sacrifice. Without love the most gifted individual is nothing, and without love the supreme sacrifice is of no profit. Love is the highest attainment to which man can ascend. "If we love one another, God dwelleth in us, and his love is perfected in us" (1 John 4:12; KJV). In Christ love is life, and life is love.

That James had this in mind is evident from what he says in dealing with the problem of showing partiality toward those who are rich and influential. He describes the universal obligation of love as "the royal law," the king of all laws (James 2:8). This

122

is the law from which all others derive their meaning and toward which all others are subservient. "If you really fulfil the royal law, according to the scripture, 'You shall love your neighbor as yourself,' you do well. But if you show partiality, you commit sin, and are convicted by the law as transgressors" (2:8, 9; RSV). Love for any neighbor precludes the showing of partiality. Partiality violates the fundamental law of social well-being as manifested in the life of Jesus.

There is another thing about the word "perfect" we should not overlook. It is a translation of *teleios*, a word meaning "completion" or "perfection." In most cases it refers to perfection for a purpose or definite end. It was used for the attainment of the goal by a runner and his reception of the honorary wreath. It was used in the scholastic realm for one who had finished his course in the academy. Thus, James wrote a law combining all of the moral and ethical values Jesus taught and exemplified, and which were designed to make a man all that God intended for him to be.

No legal code can ever accomplish this. For man there must be an ideal so majestic that it will challenge him to transcend the fleshly and carnal life. As man identifies with that ideal he rises above the temptations that beset him and he becomes more than a conqueror. The revelation of God is a mirror reflecting the face and person of Jesus, making our shortcomings manifest by contrast.

The perfect law is one of liberty. This is interesting because law is a restraining and restricting force by its very nature. But the law of Christ, the governing principles of the Christ-life, frees one from debtorship to the flesh, from the slavery of passion and inordinate desire. It frees him to become his best as a son of God. But there is more to it than that, as will be seen by a study of the use of the same expression in James 2:8-13.

We must never forget that James was writing to Jews, who were familiar with the law as given by Moses. History portrays James himself as one who rigorously kept the law. The first part of the second chapter of his letter deals with the tendency to show preference toward the rich and affluent who visited the assembly of the saints. Such a practice might well be justified by a Jew who would say, "We were simply doing what the law enjoins in showing special consideration, for we were told to love our neighbor as ourselves."

To this James replies, "If you really fulfil the royal law, according to the scripture, 'You shall love your neighbor as yourself,' you do well" (2:8). If that were the only motivation for showing politeness to visitors, there would be no distinction in the treatment of the rich and poor; but showing partiality is not obeying the law of God. It is a sin, and the one convicted of it is a transgressor. Remember that the Jews to whom James wrote had no New Testament Scriptures. When James talked about the "royal law according to the scriptures," he was quoting Leviticus 19:18.

To justify one's action by quoting one statement from the law while ignoring the remainder of it is to be guilty of inconsistency. The Jews had enumerated 613 commandments in the law. It was not conceivable to them that one could obey all of them. As a result they had developed the casuistic philosophy that one could total the commands he had kept during a certain period, and subtract the total of the ones he had specifically violated. If the result showed a favorable balance, he could feel justified. The rabbis taught that if one observed a command of the law, good was credited to him. His life would be prolonged and he would prosper in his inheritnace. James insisted that what counts is one's attitude to the whole law, not the observance of an isolated commandment, which can then be quoted to gain credit.

The follower of Jesus is not under any written code enforced with police power or judicial authority. Therefore, writes James, "So speak and so act as those who are to be judged under the law of liberty"

(2:12:RSV). We are not under statutory specifications, but in a spiritual relationship. We are to govern our speech and actions by the law of liberty, and this principle of behavior makes it possible for us to show mercy. Mercy is not required by one who lives perfectly, but by one who does not. It is the kind and compassionate treatment shown to an offender.

Law, as such, is interested in justice, not mercy. There is no justice in absolute mercy, and no mercy in absolute justice. One dies without mercy under the testimony of credible witnesses, when he is under a written code of authority. We operate under a law of liberty, and this provides for kindness or compassion. The one who shows no mercy will receive none. Our English word "mercy" is from the Latin *mercedis*, meaning payment, or reward. It refers to the heavenly reward to be given to the compassionate.

None of us will attain to glory except by the mercy of God. We simply cannot be saved upon the basis of our own righteousness. God will use the yardstick by which we measure others as the criterion for measuring us. If we show no mercy we will receive none. If we receive none we will be lost. The principle of liberty in Christ Jesus makes it possible for us to be compassionate. It distinguishes between love of law and the law of love.

126

Chapter 11

# THE COMMANDMENTS OF JESUS

Many people have not yet grasped the greatness of a covenant inscribed by the Holy Spirit upon the chambers of the heart. It is difficult for them to see the difference between the requirements of a written legal code and the commandments voiced by Jesus. They reason that if a disciple of Jesus is obligated to keep His commandments, and if those commandments are now contained in the collection of documents called the New Testament Scriptures, those Scriptures must be a written code of laws or commandments.

In plain terms, this would mean that the law of Moses was a custodian to bring us to Christ, and that Christ has now placed us under another custodian. It should be a sufficient answer to this kind of rationalization to point out that it negates everything in the very apostolic letters, which are assumed to be the new written code. Nothing can be plainer than the statement of Paul, "But now that faith has come, we are no longer under a custodian" (Galatians 3:25; RSV).

Certainly the disciples of Jesus will keep the commandments of Jesus. This is the very essence of discipleship. But keeping His commandments is the response of love to Him as a person and not the observance of a code through fear of the consequences. A lawbreaker is subject to fear, but "There is no fear in love; but perfect love casteth out fear: because fear hath torment. He that feareth is not made perfect in love. We love him, because he first loved us" (1 John 4:18, 19; KJV).

Jesus did not come to place us under law but to reconcile us to God. He came that we might have life and have it more abundantly. He came to restore a relationship that had been shattered by sin and abrogated by alienation. Thus He said, "If a man love me, he will keep my words: and my Father will love him, and we will come unto him, and make our abode with him" (John 14:23; KJV). There is no greater happiness than the recognition that one has the Father and the Son as his permanent guests.

Many people who read this would be flattered if the President of the United States chose to stay one night in their home. A far more tremendous honor comes to those who can live daily in the intimate companionship of the Creator of the universe and His only begotten Son. This transcendent experience does not begin with, nor result from, obedience to commands, as many people think. It begins with love for Jesus, and it is perpetuated and sustained by that love. Keeping the commandments of Jesus results from that love as a natural and effortless consequence. It is not conformity to a code, but the affectionate surrender to the embrace of a person in joyful recognition of acceptance.

One of the most outstanding declarations about the divine-human relationship which results from true discipleship occurs in John 15:9-15. Here Jesus is sharing His intimate thoughts with the apostles before His imminent torture and death. They were sorrowful in contemplation of the anticipated separation, but Jesus speaks of love, joy, and peace. He uses the terms "my love," "my joy," and "my peace," indicating that there was a quality about them that the world had not probed or understood. Indeed, He had said, "Peace I leave with you, my peace I give unto you: not as the world giveth, give I unto you" (14:27; KJV). He then declared that the Father is glorified when the branches He has pruned produce fruit commensurate with the care bestowed upon them. This is how men prove they are disciples of Jesus Christ. Fruit cannot be borne by branches detached from the vine, and the fruit is an indication that the branches are connected with and abiding in the vine. Abundance of fruit is proof of the response to the action of God upon the life. "Every branch that beareth fruit, he purgeth it, that it may bring forth more fruit" (15:2).

In direct connection with the statement relating to that productivity as a proof of discipleship, Jesus goes on to say, "As the Father hath loved me, so have I loved you: continue ye in my love. If ye keep my commandments, ye shall abide in my love; even as I have kept my Father's commandments, and abide in his love. These things have I spoken unto you, that my joy might remain in you, and that your joy might be full" (vv. 9-11). Keeping the commandments is here placed in a framework of divine love and joy.

Jesus was loved, so He was able to love. His love for the disciples was a projection of the love manifested toward Him by the Father. His keeping of the Father's commandment was a demonstration of His response to the Father's love. The statement, "If ye keep my commandments, ye shall continue in my love" (v. 10), is not so much a conditional stipulation as it is an explanatory statement. Keeping the commandments is the way we exhibit love. The way Jesus manifested love for us is the way we are to manifest love for Jesus.

These guidelines and criteria were spoken, not to remind us of a law, but to remind us of the divine joy that results from union with Jesus. Joy is one of God's gifts to us. It is a fruit of the Spirit. What Jesus said about keeping His commandments was to guarantee that the delight and exultation that transcend sorrow and discouragement would remain with us and fill our cup of life with gladness and rejoicing.

Jesus continues with the statement, "This is my commandment, That ye love one another, as I have loved you" (v. 12). It is noteworthy that several times in the New Covenant Scriptures a switch is made from "commandments" in the plural to "commandment" in the singular. Each time it is asserted that the commandment of Christ is to love one another. The fact that the degree of our love is measured by the love of Jesus for men makes it a new commandment. The love that sums up all other commandments is defined, not by a legalistic explanation, but by a divine attitude and action. The one who loves in this fashion fulfills the whole law; that is, he exhibits the state of righteousness for which law was designed and to which it could never attain.

This will not satisfy one who is convinced that keeping the law is the real goal of human existence and the only hope of pleasing God. To such a person love is only one tenet of a legal system; it is not the ultimate response of a broken and contrite spirit that reaches up to God to experience

131

love and reaches down to the needy in order to share it. Everyone must make a choice between love of law and the law of love, and his choice will determine whether he will exist in bondage or live in liberty.

What difference can there be between a legal system and the commandments of Jesus? This question is always posed by those who would channel and confine the grace of God until they can control it. If one is obligated by his relationship to Jesus to keep His commandments, even though he is gathered up in love, he still must be under a code of laws. But there are great areas of difference between law-keeping and the response to grace in love. We shall mention only four such areas, and these have to do primarily with the attitudes engendered by consciousness of law.

1. All written codes of law must have a recognized interpreter. The interpretation of law by such a recognized authority becomes the official one, and it must be followed, whether the individual agrees with the assigned meaning or not. The Constitution of the United States of America is the foundation of our republic, but the interpretations placed upon the provisions by the Supreme Court becomes the real law that the citizens must obey. In the two centuries since the Constitution was drafted, a great mass of material has been collected into books containing judgments, deci-

sions, rulings, and precedents. The constitutional lawyer must consult the index for all of these in order to make an appeal or a case in court.

The Roman Catholic Church is a legalistic institution. It is a religio-politico power patterned after the Roman imperial system. At the head of this sprawling "empire" is a pope, a universal "father," whose *ex cathedra* pronouncements are deemed to be infallible. They must therefore be accepted without question as the official dogma of the members. All Protestant groups regarding the New Covenant Scriptures as a legal code have their own official interpreters, and these will differ from each other according to the authoritarian structure created by the various sects.

In religious parties that are congregational in form, a "presbytery," or eldership, may be vested with the power to decide upon the official interpretation. This becomes a dogma, and from this no appeal can be taken. The spirit of dogma is the same, whether administered by a universal pope or a local eldership. It differs in degree, but not in nature. It is inherent in any movement that regards itself as under law and not under grace, or which interprets grace in terms of law.

If we regard the "new covenant" as one in which God's laws are inscribed in our hearts and written in our minds, rather

133

than compiled in a written code of jurisprudence, the individual conscience, enlightened by truth, becomes the supreme court. An institution does not have a mind. Although political, social, and religious movements operate in such a fashion as to try to produce a "mass mind" and "an organization man," this was never God's purpose. That idea runs counter to the divine design for our spiritual development. "Let every man be fully persuaded in his own mind" (Romans 14:5) is an expression of Heaven's purpose. Each individual makes the response of love to God and man according to his ability at the time.

2. Every legalistic system must create an enforcement agency. Laws not enforced are worse than no laws at all. A society based upon constitutional law must develop a police power charged with the responsibility of keeping the citizenry in line and in subjection to the law. In the Roman Catholic Church, the hierarchy is the enforcement agency. The inventions of purgatory and the confessional booth make it possible for the parish priest to entertain pleas of guilt and to assess the various penalties for infractions of the moral code.

In other religious legal systems, conformity is secured by investing the clergy or presbytery with special powers of enforcement. Under threat of expulsion from the community for any expression of opinion contrary to the established dogmata, silence is secured by coercion. Dissidents are thus kept in check. All of this is contrary to the grace-faith covenant in which an individual's relationship with God is based upon receiving Jesus as the Lord of life and continuing to abide in Him.

3. Regarding the new covenant as a system of laws contained in a written code automatically assumes that anyone who does not meticulously comply with every specification is a lawbreaker. The religious establishment will treat such persons as criminals or felons. They will be dealt with summarily, lest they influence others to engage in similar "illegal" actions. There is no room for a brother who is honestly mistaken because "ignorance of the law excuses no one."

In legalistic communities, every person who questions the *status quo* becomes a heretic or false teacher. Although the latter term is used only once in the New Covenant Scriptures, where it applies to one who denies the Lord who bought us, it is a general designation for those who disagree in modern sectarian parlance.

All of this is in contravention to our adoption into a divine family or household. In this concept, the children do not reach a common level of understanding at a given time, but continue in various stages of mental growth and achievement. Those

135

who do not fully grasp the Father's will, or who are unable to freely carry it out, are not lawbreakers. There are those who are weak in the faith, but they still are to be received (Romans 14:1). There are members of the body deemed less honorable, but upon these we bestow the more abundant honor (1 Corinthians 12:23). All of us are to walk according to our present spiritual attainment (Philippians 3:16), even as we seek to grow in grace and in knowledge of the truth.

Involuntary ignorance is not a sin, although voluntary ignorance, which is a deliberate refusal to learn, is always a sin. We can keep the commandments only as we become aware of and apprehend them. To obey them as a response to the person of Jesus provides for our loving even while we are learning. It is our love and not our degree of knowledge that makes us worthy to be received. "If anyone fancies that he knows, he knows nothing yet, in the true sense of knowing. But if a man loves, he is acknowledged by God" (1 Corinthians 8:3; NEB). We are forbidden to judge a brother upon one hand or to hold him in contempt upon the other. "Each of us must consider his neighbour and think what is for his good and will build up the common life" (Romans 15:2; NEB).

4. Another characteristic of a legalistic system is to create a feeling of insecurity

136

and doubt as to one's standing with God. No one can ever be sure at a given time that he knows as much of the law as he ought to know in order to be saved. No one knows that his obedience to what he does know is sufficient for his justification.

The keeping of the commandments as a response *of* love and a response *to* love places the emphasis upon love rather than upon the commandments. One does not love Christ because he keeps the commandments, but he keeps the commandments because he loves Christ. He does not keep the commandments in order to be received, but because he has been received he keeps the commandments.

There is always an element of fear connected with law, but perfect love casts out fear: "And we have known and believed the love that God hath to us. God is love; and he that dwelleth in love dwelleth in God, and God in him. Herein is our love made perfect, that we may have boldness in the day of judgment: because as he is, so are we in this world. There is no fear in love; but perfect love casteth out fear: because fear hath torment. He that feareth is not made perfect in love" (1 John 4:16-18; KJV).

We have the assurance that God loves us. He proved it by sending His Son to be the atonement for our sins. We know that even death cannot be triumphant over us. God will give us victory over the last enemy through our Lord Jesus Christ. Even now we can cast our cares, concerns, and worries upon Him, because He cares for us. He has promised that He will never leave or forsake us. We are not foster children delivered to God's house by law. We are sons and daughters of the Lord Almighty. He is our Father and we are His children.

We study the New Covenant Scriptures, not to prepare ourselves as lawyers, but to know better how to express love for God and our neighbors. We regard the love letters of the apostles as did those to whom they were originally written. We read them as letters from dear friends and not as a compendium of laws sent from a bureau of statutory requirements. Even those letters dealing with thorny problems use the word "brothers" repeatedly. The apostles were not writing to brothers-in-law, but to brothers in love.

There are warm and intimate communications that close with such words as "My love be with you all in Christ Jesus" (1 Corinthians 16:24; KJV). Why should we take these and convert them into cold, legalistic documents, thus building up walls of hostility between us? Did the saints in Philippi, who were addressed by Paul as "my brethren dearly beloved and longed for, my joy and crown" (4:1), subject the letter they received to laws of interpretation and hermeneutics, or did they read it with tears of gladness coursing down their cheeks? Did those to whom John wrote as "my little children" regard his letter as a legal document to be debated as in a tribunal, or as a letter to be read in the family?

When Paul learned from Chloe and her family of the crisis faced by the congregation at Corinth, should he have written, "Whereas an emergency exists for the immediate taking effect of this act, the same shall be in full force and effect from and after its passage"? As it was he wrote, "I write not these things to shame you, but as my beloved sons I warn you" (1 Corinthians 4:14; KJV). He declared that Timothy and he had no "dominion over your faith, but are helpers of your joy: for by faith ye stand" (2 Corinthians 1:24). Why can we not regard these wonderful letters as a help and encouragement to our joy, rather than as documents written to exercise dominion over our faith?

"When you seek to be justified by way of law, your relation with Christ is completely severed: you have fallen out of the domain of God's grace. For to us, our hope of attaining that righteousness which we eagerly await is the work of the Spirit through faith. If we are in union with Christ Jesus, circumcision makes no difference at all, nor does the want of it; the only thing that counts is faith active in love" (Galatians 5:4-6; NEB).

Chapter 12

# SUMMARY AND CONCLUSION

Perhaps it will help us all to put into condensed form what was presented in the previous chapters. We can thus re-examine the points of emphasis and determine if they have validity in the light of God's revelation. Although no one likes to regiment thinking, in this instance it may be of some assistance to number the pertinent points for the purpose of studying them in more orderly fashion.

1. In His association with mankind, God has revealed himself as a covenant-making personality. He said to Noah and his sons, "I will establish my covenant with you" (Genesis 9:11; KJV). He said to Abraham, "I will make my covenant between me and thee" (Genesis 17:2). This means that God exhibited a willingness to enter into an agreement with men. He was willing to bind himself to perform certain things, based upon the immutability inherent in a divine promise and upon the integrity involved in His character and name.

Because of these things, our relationship to God must be a covenantal relationship.

The nature of that relationship will be regulated by the covenant that creates it. In every case the covenant people will differ from those who are not under the covenant. They will be a special people because God has entered into a special agreement, the terms of which set them apart from other people.

2. There are two covenants in history that are of significance because of their relationship to Christ. The first of these two covenants was made with the twelve tribes of Isarel, and it constituted them into a nation. That nation was to keep alive the concept of monotheism until Christ could be manifested in the flesh as the Son of God. This first covenant consisted of Ten Commandments, which were written on two tablets of stone. It was delivered to Moses on Mount Sinai and became the constitution of a nation composed of "the people of God."

The covenant inaugurated a legalistic regime, and was supplemented by laws, statutes, judgments, and commandments, all of which were compiled in a book. The book was sprinkled with the blood of a sacrifice and designated "the book of the covenant" (Exodus 24:7). In spite of severe penalties for violating this written code, the people refused to be guided by its provisions. Finally, God announced that He would make a new covenant (Jeremiah

31:31-33). Unlike the one made when Israel was freed from Egypt, the laws and requirements of the new relationship were not to be recorded externally, but were to be internally inscribed and written on the hearts of men (v. 33).

The covenant made at Mount Horeb, or Sinai, was designated the "first covenant" (Hebrews 8:7) and the "old covenant" (Hebrews 8:13). The "new covenant," which created a personal rather than a national relationship with God, was declared to be "a better covenant, which was established upon better promises" (8:6). The apostle Paul introduces an interesting allegory, in which the covenants are likened to Hagar and Sarah, both of whom bore children to Abraham. The allegory points up the truth that those under the "first covenant" were in legal bondage, but those under the "new covenant" are free (Galatians 4:21-31). Regarding the law as a yoke of slavery, he encourages those under the new covenant to "stand fast therefore in the liberty wherewith Christ hath made us free, and be not entangled again with the yoke of bondage" (Galatians 5:1; KJV).

The purpose of the legalistic covenant was to keep God's people under surveillance and strict control in order to bring them to Christ. The coming of Christ was designed to bring man into a completely new relationship with God, a relationship

142

of faith. The type of relationship that was instituted through Moses stands in stark contrast to that which came through Christ. "The law was given by Moses, but grace and truth came by Jesus Christ" (John 1:17; KJV).

There is as much difference between the relationship that was previously enforced and that which we now enjoy with God, as there is between a legal code and undeserved kindness. All law is a restraining and restrictive influence. Law is intended to define boundaries, to restrict liberties, and to provide penalties. Under law man is really under guard. So the apostle writes, "But before faith came, we were kept under the law, shut up unto the faith which should afterwards be revealed" (Galatians 3:23; KJV). In this rendering by the *King James Version* the words "kept" and "shut up" are significant. The first is a term meaning to be under guard; the second is used of those who are confined in a stockade or prison.

In the next verse, the law is defined as a "child-conductor" or "custodian" (in the *Revised Standard Version*). The ultimate purpose was to deliver God's people to Christ. In Christ a custodian is no longer needed. Here we are kept by the love of God and are sharers in a life that no law could ever give (3:21). The glorious covenantal relationship now sustained is not based upon

143

a written code at all. We ourselves become the letter of Christ. The new covenant is not written with ink, but with the Spirit of the living God. It is not written on tablets of stone or other external material, but upon the tablets of the heart (2 Corinthians 3:3). The new covenant is not one of a written code, but of the Spirit.

There are but two approaches to justification, or righteousness, that is made available to man. Justification is a state of guiltlessness in the presence of God. It is regarded as righteousness because it restores a right relationship with the Father, a relationship that had been broken up by sin and transgression. Justification is available upon either of two conditions: law or faith. There is no other ground for hope.

While justification is available on these two bases, it is impossible to attain by law because of man's weakness in the flesh. Justification by law demands perfect conformity with law. Whatever law man regards as the basis of justification must be meticulously obeyed. The least infraction or deviation ends all hope of justification and spells disaster. The very principle of attempted justification by law is that one lives only as long as he does exactly what the law demands. "The man which doeth these things shall live by them" (Romans 10:5; KJV). Law as a means of life becomes a way of death.

144

3. After fifteen centuries of dealing with man in a legalistic covenantal arrangement, God sent His Son into the world. He was sent to condemn sin in the flesh and to institute a new and living way under which man would be justified by faith. This Jesus accomplished through His own sacrifice on Calvary. It is the atoning blood of Jesus that makes possible the forgiveness of our sins, and removes the guilt and stain of sin under which we would otherwise rest. The faith that justifies is not faith in a system, a ritual, or a code. Faith involves trust, and the faith that justifies and restores the right relationship with God is absolute trust in Jesus' atonement. Every person has sinned and come short of the glory of God (Romans 3:23). No one can be justified in God's sight by deeds of law. Justification upon the basis of human law-keeping is an impossibility. Law produces knowledge of sin, but cannot produce a sense of righteousness. Therefore the righteousness of God is not based upon legal conformity.

Accordingly, the righteousness of God has been made known as available to man on other terms. It is "the righteousness of God which is by faith" (Romans 3:22). Under it we are "justified freely by his grace through the redemption that is in Christ Jesus" (3:24). To be justified is to be guiltless. None of us can attain to this state. All are guilty before God. But under

145

the new covenant of grace, which reaches its apex in the atonement by the blood of Christ, God declares us guiltless. His declaration is made, not upon the basis of our deeds, but upon the ground of the sacrifice made for us by His Son who bore our guilt upon the cross.

Righteousness is not a state that we strive to attain by the laborious and self-defeating method of acquiring knowledge and implementing it by human effort. It is by divine declaration as a manifestation of marvelous grace and mercy. When one ceases to trust in his own righteousness, trusting absolutely and without reservation in "that which is through the faith of Christ, the righteousness which is of God by faith" (Philippians 3:9), his faith is counted to him for righteousness. He is justified by faith, declared guiltless by the Father, and treated thus.

4. Galatians 3:22 reveals the fact that the Scripture "concluded all under sin." "All" includes the whole world, those who had the law of God and those who were without law. Everyone was in the same lost state, so that all could equally qualify for the right relationship God had conditioned upon trust in the righteousness of faith in Christ Jesus. The law was simply a custodian to bring those under its care to Jesus who is the justifier of all. With the coming of faith in Christ as the basis of righteous-

ness, law was terminated as a system of seeking justification. "For Christ is the end of the law for righteousness to every one that believeth" (Romans 10:4; KJV).

This means that our acceptance of the good news of the grace of God is not upon the basis of obedience to law. It is not by meritorious works performed in a kind of barter system. We do not trade our effort for a reward. We do not deposit our good deeds in a heavenly vending machine and await the desired result to come tumbling down. Paul tells us, "Ye are all the children of God by faith in Christ Jesus. For as many of you as have been baptized into Christ have put on Christ" (Galatians 3:26, 27; KJV). Faith is not a work demanded by law, for if it were we would still be under a custodian. Baptism is not an act of law. It is simply faith activated. It is demonstrated and manifested in the only way that vital faith in Christ can be shown: by loving response to His example and will.

Here we have a great contrast between human reactions under the two divergent covenants of law and grace. We are conditioned in our social culture to a world of "law and order." The latter (grace) is seemingly dependent upon the former (law). Therefore, many sincere disciples of Christ are afraid to even think of our not being under a written code. To them it means that everyone must make the choice between law or lawlessness. But there is no spirit of lawlessness in Christ. Here the contrast is between law and love. There can be no anarchy in Christ Jesus for the simple reason that all of His subjects have surrendered their will to His, and He is Lord of all!

The very Scriptures that some would like to regard as law specifically declare, "The law is not made for the righteous man, but for the lawless and disobedient, for the ungodly and for sinners, for unholy and profane, . . ." (1 Timothy 1:9). In Christ Jesus we are made partakers of the divine nature. We are in the world but not of it. We no longer walk according to the flesh but according to the Spirit. We are not under condemnation. We have been set free from the law of sin and death.

Our obedience is not to a written code but to a loving Savior. His commandments do not constitute "laying down the law" for us, but a lifting up to love. Our compliance is not conformity to a code but the response of love to a person. He said, "If a man love me, he will keep my words" (John 14:23). It is just that simple. I repent because I love Him. I confess my sins because I love Him. I ask forgiveness because I love Him. I do not want to hurt Him, I want to be close to Him. I want to be His, and I want Him to be mine. Our relationship would not be enhanced by law, but destroyed by it.

This brings us to the most difficult part in sharing my concept of our relationship with God created by the new covenant. It is that of my own experience. Most of us are aware of the fact that it is easier to deal with such a theme academically than to lay bare the inmost feelings of one's own heart. For years I struggled to please God on the basis of conformity to a written code. I regarded the apostolic letters as a compilation of judgments, statutes, and judicial requirements. I felt that these demanded perfect obedience under threat of eternal condemnation.

Since I had been taught that we were under "the new law," I began with that presupposition, and everything that was written I interpreted within that frame of reference. Accordingly, grace became merely another vehicle through which law was conveyed. Faith was to be used as the grappling-hook by which one scaled the steep side of the mountain as he agonized upward toward God. Present always within one who takes this mental route is the sense of his own failure. He is not righteous by his own makeshift criterion, and he knows that he is not.

In order to live with oneself under such a system it is necessary to engage in casuistry, and this amounts to self-deception. The person selects some items with which he can relate and invests them with an aura of importance, which really belongs to the total relationship. By emphasizing these and maintaining a degree of loyalty in their defense, he flatters himself that he is faithful to God. What this does, of course, is to lead him into a frightful state of self-righteousness. He becomes a worshiper of his own mental and moral powers, and demonstrates his insecurity by aggressive assaults upon others.

I have been delivered from the fears, inhibitions, and hostilities, which seem to be the natural result of confinement. I am free to examine the marvelous revelation of God in a new and open way. I marvel at the fact that God, sinless and perfect, was willing to enter into a covenant with me, as sinful and imperfect as I am. I rejoice in it, even though I can neither fully comprehend or explain it. The divine agreement by which I became a son of God is written in my heart by the Holy Spirit. My own heart is an "ark of the covenant." It is here God dwells through the divine Comforter or Helper.

I read the New Covenant Scriptures now with the eyes of my understanding being enlightened. They are more precious to me and I have a deeper sense of hunger for their content. I regard the letters of the envoys for what they are: letters of love written to those caught up in the human predicament. They were written to assure those people that they have eternal life. They are letters of correction, admonition, and exhortation. They were never intended to develop legal or technical specialists, but lovers of God and men. They speak to me with new depth and power.

I look at life with a new sense of its meaning, since I realize that eternal life was embodied in Christ Jesus, and through Him we share in that wonderful transcendent dimension of existence. He has put all history into proper focus for me, including the agony as well as the ecstasy. Eternal life is to know God and His Son, to experience a creative relationship with them, which, even though it entails suffering here, will result in glory.

I face death as the "great adventure," the final transforming and transferring event, the gateway to eternal rest, the door to peace in its ultimate. Hope becomes a greater comfort when one realizes that it never disappoints because the love of God is poured out in our hearts by the Holy Spirit. Perfect love casts out fear, and that includes the fear of death.

When I came to accept the reality of the indwelling Spirit as God's immeasurable gift to us during the absence of His Son, the significance of the covenant of grace, as opposed to a legalistic contract such as was given by Moses, became immediately apparent. I was no longer lonely. I never felt

151

forsaken. I could rejoice in the face of calamity and triumph over adversity. My prayers became more intimate, my concern for others grew deeper.

The fact is that God has accepted and received me as I am, and I do not have to struggle for recognition. This truth has stifled any sense of rivalry with others. We do not need to compete for the favor of the Father. There is room for all of us under the umbrella of divine affection. All who have entered the family through faith are brothers and sisters. I am free to be as merciful toward them as God has been toward me. Each must be allowed to stand or fall to his own Master. Each must be fully persuaded in his own mind.

It is a blessing beyond compare to realize that we are "dead indeed unto sin, but alive unto God through Jesus Christ our Lord" (Romans 6:11). We are dead and our lives are hid with Christ in God. When Christ who is our life shall appear, then shall we also appear with Him in glory. (See Colossians 3:3, 4). No wonder it is written, "Every man that hath this hope in him purifieth himself, even as he is pure" (1 John 3:3). It is all summed up for me in one glowing statement, as it appears in the *Revised Standard Version:* "For sin will have no dominion over you, since you are not under law but under grace" (Romans 6:14). Praise God!